Weird Cars

By John A. Gunnell

"Things the Motorist Wants to Know" 1911 vision of 1961 Car.

Robert J. Gary of Stevens Point, Wisconsin gave us this illustration of a weird-looking car that he clipped from a Ford advertisement in the days that he worked for Ford Motor Company. The vehicle depicted in the ad is a 1911 artist's "vision" of what a 1961 automobile would look like. The Volkwagen-like front end is not far off reality, but the rest of the vehicle is a far cry from what people were tooling around in during 1961.

Published by:

krause
publications

700 E. State Street • Iola, WI 54990-0001
Telephone: 715/445-2214

Library of Congress Number: 93-77540

ISBN: 0-87341-253-2

Printed in the United States of America

Contents

Weird Cars from A to Z!

Credits 4

Introduction 6

Artistic Autos 10

Buses 20

    Corvair Ultra Van 26

Custom Cars 28

Double Ended Cars 46

Eccentric Cars 51

    Sir Vival has Survived the Years 57

    Tucker: Birth and Death of an Innovative Automobile 60

    Stout Years Ahead With Scarab 64

Factory Show Cars 69

    Chrysler's Weird Turbine Car 74

    Ghost Pontiac 80

    Ford's Brightest Idea: The Stainless Steel Cars 88

Giant-Sized Cars 96

    The Longest Car In The World 103

Hot Rods 105

Imports 109

    Tatraplan: Czech Rarity 117

Jaunty Jalopies 123

Kooky Kars 129

    The Bowling Pin Car 130

    Santa's Rocket Revisited 133

    Did He Trade in His Sleigh? 134

    Louie Mattar's Non-stop Cadillac 138

Little Cars 141

    Short Car was a Long Time in the Making 152

Movie Cars & Media Mobiles 154

    Green Hornet's Black Beauty Has Changed Over the Years 160

    Holy Hubcaps! It's the Batmobile 164

    Hollywood's Great Race Fun, But Not Authentic 170

Neo-Classic Automobiles 186

Owner Modified Cars 193

Product Mobiles 202

    Land Cruiser and Boat Cars by Bud 207

    Hot-doggin' Through History 218

Quads 224

Racing Cars 231

    Ab Jenkins and His Mormon Meteors 238

Ski-mobiles and Swim-mobiles 241

    Virgil White's Snow Vehicles Were Fords 242

    Soviets Preserve Lenin's Autos 244

    Unusual Citröen 245

Three-Wheel Cars 251

    Remember The Davis? 252

Ultra Streamliners 259

Vans 267

    Going "Ape" for a Good Cause 271

Weird Working Vehicles 272

    How Do You Spell Relief? They Spelled It "Labatt's" 274

X-Perimental Cars 281

    The Octoauto 285

Yank Tank 293

    Snow Cruiser: It's All Yours: Go Get It 294

Zany Cars 297

Dedication

This book is dedicated to Jesse Gunnell who is turning into a real car enthusiast during his 13th year. May he always enjoy automobiles and may they always make him smile like the vehicles in WEIRD CARS will make you smile.

Cover and Photo Credits

Afrons Pulling Team: 240 (bottom). American Motors Corporation: 77. American Motors Owners Association: 229 (top). Atlanta Motor Speedway: 228 (top), 240. Auburn-Cord-Dusenburg Museum: 18 (top), 212 (bottom), 215 (top), 288. Automobile Club of America, Incorporated: 103, 104. James Bach: 62 (top). William L. Bailey: 63 (top), 146 (top), 284 (bottom), 292 (bottom). Don Baker: 300 (bottom). George W. Barber: 233. Barnes Thunderbird Shop: 201 (top). Barris Kustom Industries: 96, 97, 98 (top), 154, 155, 159 (bottom), 177. Jim Benjaminson: 220 (top), 223 (top). Blackhawk Classic Automobile Collection: 95 (top), 259, 266. John Boniface 210 (bottom); Joe Bortz: 69. Bernie Brown: 278 (bottom). Buick Motor Division: 79. Ken Buttolph: 44 (top), 195 (bottom). Bob Butts: 42, 136 (bottom), 137, 158 (top), 165, 175, 176, 178, 179, 180, 181, 182, 183, 184, 189 (bottom), 268 (top). John & Carol Calvert: 230 (top). Camelot Classics: 189 (top). Phillip C. Campbell: 194 (top). Chevrolet Motor Division: 78 (top). Chicago Antique Historical Automobile Museum: 100 (bottom), 156 (top), 159 (top), 160, 162 (top). Chrysler Corporation: 70, 72, 73, 74, 136 (top), 99, 270 (bottom). Henry Austin Clark, Jr.: 142, 285, 287 (top). Classic Car Club of America: 239 (bottom). College Place Lions Club: 197. Collins Industries, Incorporated: 26. Custom Cloud Motors: 30 (top). Carl H. Davis: 88, 89, 90, 93. D. James Dee: 18 (bottom). James M. Degnan: 277. Jerry DiDonato: 56, 57, 58. Walt Disney Productions: 109. Ed Dooley: 98 (bottom), 99 (top). Dunham Coach: 190 (bottom). Paul & Lucille Durbin: 48 (top). David S. Ebersole: 203, 210 (top), 213 (top). Lewis W. Ediger: 26. Extravaganza Limos, Incorporated: 301. Fantasy Cars, Incorporated: 42, 136 (bottom), 137, 158 (top), 165, 175, 176, 178, 179, 180, 181, 182, 183, 184, 189 (bottom), 268 (top). Don Fest: 267, 271. Ford Motor Company: 72. Charles and Dawnita Forell: 101. Leo Frank: 194 (bottom). Robert L. Frissore: 215 (bottom). Robert Frumpkin: 110, 135, 196. Ken Fuertsch: 28 (bottom), 29, 38 (bottom), 39, 40, 41. FWD Corp.: 229 (bottom). General Motors Corporation: 71, 72, 224, 225, 236. Jeff Gibson: 152. Gilmore Oil Company: 157 (top). Bill Glass (House of Hubcaps): 199 (bottom). Dan W. Golden: 270 (top). B.F. Goodrich: 227 (top). Goodyear Tire & Rubber Company: 20, 21, 79, 228 (bottom), 293, 294, 295, 296. Grand Prix Museum: 129. GreatRace Ltd.: 63 (bottom), 66, 168 (bottom). Group Promotions: 163, 164, 165. Albert Guibara: 10, 11, 12. Cynthia Ann Gunnell: 112 (bottom). John A. Gunnell: 28 (top), 29, 32, 36, 45, 50 (bottom), 64, 78 (bottom), 84, 85, 86, 87 (bottom), 99 (bottom), 100 (top), 108, 162 (bottom), 199 (bottom), 226 (bottom), 235 (bottom), 237, 238 (top), 239 (top), 279. Harrah's Automobile Collection: 108, 168 (top), 232 (top), 264, 265. Beverly Hillbillies: 123. Tom & Nancy Hoefert: 24 (bottom), 280 (bottom). Ted Holden: 49 (bottom). Stephen ("Hoop") Hooper: Cover (1941 Packard funeral hearse) 14, 15, 16, 17. Honda Motor Car Company: 95 (bottom). "Doc" Howell: 50 (top). Vic Hyde: 251 (bottom). Imperial Palace Auto Collection: 35, 54 (bottom), 55 (bottom), 157 (bottom), 186, 187, 250 (top). Indianapolis Motor Speedway Corporation: 206, 207, 208, 209, 238. International Automobiles: 190 (bottom). Iola Old Car Show: 55 (top), 122 (top), 153 (bottom). Gordon Istenes: 49 (top). Mel Jameson: 263 (bottom), 269 (bottom), 290 (top, center). Elustra S.J. Johnson: 192. Richard L. Knudson: 211 (top); 220 (bottom). Ron Kowalke: 34. Labatt's: 272, 273, 274. Sam LaRoue: 214 (top). John Lee: 13 (top), 19. Levy Ventures: 107 (top). Bob Loffelbein: 138, 139. General William Lyons Collection: 191 (bottom). Gene Makrancy: 88, 91. Manson/Marks: 200. Manufacturers Hanover Trust: 297, 298, 299, 300 (top). Wilfred E. Markey: Cover (Moxiemobile); 203; 213. Milwaukee Journal: 212 (top). Joe Minghenelli (Meineke Muffler): 203, 222. MoPar Action (Cliff Gromer): 231 (top), 235 (top). Motor Age: 149. Motor Bus Society: 22 (bottom), 23. Motor Vehicle Manufacturers Association: 53, 290 (bottom). Mr. Gasket Company: 106. National Automobile History Collection: 54 (top), 143, 144, 145 (bottom), 147 (top), 148 (top), 282 (bottom), 284, 287 (bottom), 289 (bottom), 291. National Bowling Hall of Fame & Museum: 130, 131. Old Cars (Weekly): 11, 25 (bottom), 33, 37, 43, 44 (bottom), 46, 47, 51, 75, 82, 83, 102, 105, 111, 113, 114, 115, 116, 121, 122 (bottom), 140 (top), 146 (bottom), 153 (top), 193, 198, 204, 213 (bottom), 226, 227 (bottom), 250 (bottom), 268 (bottom), 278 (top), 285, 289 (top). Oscar-Mayer Foods Corporation: Cover (Wienermobile), 202, 216 (top), 217, 218, 219. Owens Corning Glass Company: 68. Ron Paetz: 280 (bottom). Panther Motor Cars: 191 (top). Passport Transport: 158 (bottom), 167 (top). R.L. Patterson: 108 (top). Cameron Peck Collection (Photos by Don McCray): 124, 125, 126, 127. Colin Peck: 31. Kenneth Pepka: 223 (bottom). Richard D. Peters: 211 (bottom), 221 (top). Bill Pettit: 195 (top). Joe C. Pickett: 276 (top). Richard Pollard: 276 (bottom). Pontiac Motor Division: 69, 76, 80, 81, 94 (bottom). Frank Potter: 150 (bottom). Wally Rank: 87 (top). Rearview Mirror Museum: 108. William M. Saeman: 188. R. Schultz: 52 (top). Dennis Schrimpf: 132 (top), 134. Hayden Shepley: 148 (bottom). Silver Springs Attractions: 62 (bottom). Sothebey's: 25 (top). Special-Interest Autos: 282 (top). Margaret Tideman Sprenger: 145 (top). Standard Catalog of American Cars: 128 (top), 150 (bottom), 151, 247, 248, 249, 260, 261, 262, 263 (top). Brooks Stevens Design Associates: 24 (top), 30 (bottom), 269 (top), 283. Richard E. Strand: 197. Frank Taylor: 169, 170, 171, 172, 173, 174. Bob Temple: 117, 118, 119. Lloyd C. Texley: 203, 220, 221 (bottom). Tombstone Pizza: 214 (bottom). Tucker Motor Car Company: 59, 60. United Artists: 166. Universal Studios Incorporated: 167 (bottom). J.H. Valentine: 292 (top). Vasare: 22 (top). Veedol Starparade: Cover (Golden Arrow, Chrysler Newport Phaeton, LaBourdette Rolls-Royce, Stage Coach car), 94 (top), 112 (top), 232 (bottom), 234, 245. Volkswagen United States, Inc.: 300 (bottom). Volo Antique Auto Museum: 13 (bottom). Don Wood: 185, 241, 281, 297, 298, 299 (top), 300 (top), 302. Wally Wray: 52 (bottom), 61, 128 (bottom), 132 (bottom), 133, 140 (bottom), 141, 230 (bottom), 251 top, 252, 253, 254, 256, 257, 258. Wally Wyss: 38 (top). Whiskey Pete's Casino: 156 (bottom). George Zachman: 48 (bottom). Steven D. Zwack: 201 (bottom).

Thanks

Krause Publications appreciates the generous photographic contributions from the above sources and many other additional sources. We also extend our thanks to the OLD CARS (WEEKLY) contributors who originally authored the articles reprinted in this book. They are identified within bylines or notes included in each story. Note that some articles have been edited to include updated facts and newly discovered photos. Others who gave us advice, suggestions and information included Robert Lichty, Vincent Ruffalo, Dennis Peterson and Terry V. Boyce. We have made every effort to correctly identify photos and credit sources. Additional information regarding facts and photographs used in this book should be sent to the publisher. Please note that many excellent photographic contributions were received after the deadline for this book. Some of these may appear in additional titles that Krause Publication's Automotive Books Department plans to produce in the near future. For a catalog of all our hobby books write to: Krause Publications, 700 East State Street, Iola, Wisconsin 54990.

As anyone involved in the fascinating field of automotive history knows, every car has a story behind it. Since the vehicles pictured in this book tend to be a little bit stranger than most, the stories behind them are that much more interesting. Here's a couple of examples to introduce you to the world of weird cars:

Let There be Light

Ralph A. Ehrhardt sends this photo of a "weird" auto that served a special purpose. It is a General Electric lighting test car. The 1936 Buick was used for evaluating various types of headlights. Obviously, all would not be "on" at one time. The idea was to drive on system "A," then switch to system "B" and so on. Mr. Ehrhardt works for GE Lighting in Cleveland, Ohio and lives in Hudson, Ohio.

General Electric lighting test car.

Value Van

This photo comes from Krause Publication's numismatic (coin-collecting) publications and shows the world-famous Penny Van. The 1962 Ford Econoline is covered from bumper-to-bumper with about 48,773 pennies. The dashboard is covered with 1962-dated cents. It was built by "Penny Van Man" George King, who resembles Abraham Lincoln. In February, 1993 he sold the vehicle to Ripley's Believe It or Not. They planned to ship it to Tokyo where it would be put on permanent display with other oddities.

The world-famous "Penny Car."

Check the rest of the pages in this book for more weird car photos and stories.

WEIRD CARS

Ever since horseless carriages first hit the streets, people have met the challenges associated with creating cars by stretching their minds to the limit. When their thinking expanded in one direction, some wonderfully practical cars resulted. However, when things went the other way, some absolutely weird contraptions evolved.

The 1912 Swan Car was created for an eccentric Englishman living in Calcutta, India. (Illustration by John Gunnell)

The latter may have been the case, in 1895, when C.A. Ames pushed a mechanic to build him a car for the famous *CHICAGO TIMES-HERALD* race. Fighting a short deadline (which they missed), the two men simply hung a wooden box between two bicycles and added a pair of small steam engines. The result is what may easily have been the first "weird car."

It would not be the last one!

Four years later, Uriah Smith, of Battle Creek, Michigan, came along to take up the battle with people who claimed that noisy, smelly motor cars were spooking their horses. Smith developed the Horsey Horseless, a gas-engined buggy with the wood-carved shoulders, neck and head of a horse attached to its front end. He suggested that the sight of this car would be less shocking to livestock and that the hollow horse statue could also be used as a fuel tank.

A number of other early cars, such as the 1902 Allen, 1903 Dollwet and 1908 Penn were automotive oddities of different sorts. But, to a degree, their idiosyncrasies were more directly related to the experimental nature of the automobile of that time. Back then, there was no such thing as a "conventional" car, so there were no rules to break.

The same could not be said about R.N. Matthewson's bird-brained creation of 1912. An English eccentric living in Calcutta, India, Matthewson special ordered a sedan from his homeland that had a body shaped like a swan. The large swan's head sculpted above the radiator came with a beak that opened. Inside was an eight-pipe organ and keyboard that produced lifelike hissing sounds.

While horse cars or swan cars are as likely to appear today as they were 80 years ago, it still seems that each era of automotive development added new oddball ideas to the world of weird cars. From 1912 to 1919, there were numerous examples of vehi-

The Pep Life Savers productmobile was built on a 1934 Dodge truck chassis. (Illustration by John Gunnell)

cles reflecting an inventive spirit with their unorthodox approaches toward "building a better mousetrap."

Despite growing standardization in everyday automobiles, the auto oddities of the teens seemed to focus on changing basic rules of car building. The 1911 Reeves Octoauto questioned how many wheels a car needed and wound up with eight of them. However, a year later, Reeves introduced the Sextoauto with only six wheels. In the 1916 Serpentina, the "normal" number of four wheels was employed, but, they were arranged in an abnormal diamond-shaped pattern. Long before the seagoing Amphicar of the 1960s, the 1916 Delia and 1917 Hydrocar amphibians challenged whether automobiles should be landlubbers.

By the 1920s, the automobile had become almost an appliance to many families, but efforts to tinker with its conventional technology continued. The 1922 Reese Aero-

The '30s brought weird-looking streamliners. The teardrop car made for auto parts company McQuay-Norris toured the U.S. (Illustration by John Gunnell)

car used a rear-mounted screw propeller to wring 60-mile-per-hour speeds from a six-horsepower engine. The McLaughlin, built during 1926 in Bangor, Maine, was a larger car that used the same principle. It also came with a toboggan device that attached to the front end for snow travel. This decade also brought many cars of unusually small size, such as the Little Mystery and Martin Dart.

Among weird new trends of the 1920s, we find the earliest productmobiles. These are cars designed to promote businesses with bodies shaped like the products their owners were making or selling. There were shoe-shaped cars, candy roll cars and bowling pin cars, to name a few. A spin-off was a fleet of Bevo Boats. These were Pierce-Arrows with nautical-inspired coachwork used to promote Anheuser-Busch Company's non-alcoholic Bevo beverage during Prohibition. There was also the loco-motive-like 1922 Owens, inspired by the "You gotta have a gimmick" philosophy of a St. Paul, Minnesota car salesman.

Since cars shaped like other things seemed to give folks a blast in the 1920s, the Hungerford brothers, of Elmira, New York, created a "dynamite" land rocket. Inside this 1921 Chevrolet-based creation that Jules Verne would have been proud of, they installed a rocket engine. The 1929 Hungerford Rocket Car, which still exists, was likely the only vehicle of its type ever licensed to drive on the streets.

Although a lot of previous weirdness carried over into the 1930s (for example, the first Weinermobiles were built), a new trend was a fascination with radically stream-lined auto bodies. There had been earlier cars with torpedo tails designed to help cheat the wind, but the streamliners of the 1930s pushed the teardrop-shaped enve-lope body into strange new visual frontiers. The rapid transition from box-shaped to bullet-shaped was associated with several influences.

One influence was the emergence of industrial design as a new discipline that put more emphasis on the styling of automobiles. Americans had also been smitten with air travel and tales of science fiction. Buck Roger's planet-hopping Hollywood space-ship could hardly hold a weird flickering light to the far-out appearances of cars like the 1936 Aerocoupe, 1936 Bridges, 1937 Cricket and 1934 Holtom, as well as the bet-ter-known Dymaxion, Phantom Corsair and Stout Scarab.

During the 1940s, flying cars and safety vehicles became the trendsetters in the world of wacky wheels. Moulton B. Taylor, an aviation enthusiast, built about a dozen airplane-cars over a 20-year period. His 1948 Aero Car, with detachable wings that could be pulled behind it like a trailer, is probably the best known. Consolidated Vul-tee Aircraft Corporation's 1947 ConvAircar was another similar vehicle. There was also the high-flying Roadable of 1947, the 1949 Taylor-Dunn and the 1947 Plane-mobile.

An emphasis on safety underlaid such postwar oddities as the 1948 Gordon-Diamond, Cornell-Owning's first Safti-Car (actually a modified prewar Stout Scarab) and the three-wheel Davis of 1947. Safety features were also an integral part of the 1948 Tucker Torpedo, which may be the ultimate of all weird cars and is certainly the best publicized.

Flying cars, mini-cars, streamliners, safety vehicles and alternative-power cars continued to appear as expressions of automotive individuality during the 1950s. Added to the parade of peculiarities were electric-powered shopper vehicles. These golf cart-like machines were based on a change in lifestyle that increased the number of two-car families. With the growth of suburbia and more leisure time, many folks needed a backup vehicle to run errands or drive around town when the big car was away. Dozens of shoppers, mostly electric-powered and many with three wheels, were offered. They failed to catch on.

The decade of the 1950s also stands as the high point for factory show cars or concept vehicles. These were generally strange-looking futuristic "dream cars" and often intentionally looked weird. Their purpose was to attract attention from the public. In this book, we will feature only the strangest examples that had little possibility of ever reaching the production line.

Cars personalized by their owners stand out as the 1960s most important contribution to weirdness on wheels. This was a decade of youth and youthful expressiveness. Nearly every teenager owned his or her own car and strived to make it look different with accessories and special paint jobs. Psychedelicized Volkswagens, customized travel vans, dune buggies and school buses converted into motorhomes raised eyebrows and social consciousness levels.

In contrast to the freethinking, freewheeling '60s, the 1970s brought a decade of conservative, unexciting automobiles. New laws governing safety and antipollution equipment dictated design criteria and even restricted how private owners could modify their own vehicles. Cars and fuel grew more expensive, further inhibiting automotive creativity. Even Detroit automakers cut back on innovations to devote their corporate resources to meeting the new rules.

Beyond Detroit, the goals of tinkerers, inventors and backyard builders changed, too. They began to focus on new materials and alternative power sources. Any weird features seen in the 1970s generally boiled down to what cars were made of and what was under the hood. Creativity was chiefly inspired by the promise of rich rewards for anyone able to solve the problems that the established industry faced.

Some rather outlandish solutions evolved. In Madison, Wisconsin, seaplane builder Bruce Mohs developed two cars that were richly and refreshingly peculiar. The Mohs Ostentatienne Opera Sedan had a crush-proof hinged roof that served as its only door. If the car rolled over, the interior would retain its integrity. However, there was no way to get out if the overturned car caught on fire.

A second vehicle, called the Mohs SafariKar, had massively strong, sliding side doors. Its most unusual feature was the foam-padded Naugahyde covering the outside of the body. Both cars were built on an International truck chassis, which meant they were extremely large and had huge, oversized tires. Another car of the 1970s featuring a Naugahyde-clad body was the Ruger sports car, built by the Connecticut firearms company.

Rules and regulations affected even more creative spirits during the 1980s. In addition to major automakers, smaller firms such as Excalibur and Avanti were brought into fuller compliance with federal motor vehicle standards. In the weird car category, most activity was concentrated into the area of vehicle converters, customizers and restylers who modified standard products in socially (and legally) acceptable ways. While designed to enhance the appearance of Detroit products, some of the transformations were garish enough to please Dr. Strangelove.

The 1980s also inspired some artistic creativity that used the automobile as a medium for self-expression. Painters and sculptors decorated their vehicles with murals and artifacts that changed them into rolling artworks. One artist turned his Mustang convertible into a hippopotamus rigged up with a wagging tail and mock hippo droppings. Another installed a diorama of the Seattle, Washington skyline on the roof of his vintage Corvair.

At this point, it is too early to guess what the 1990s will add to the long tradition of wackiness on wheels. We can only hope that it continues and that this book inspires more dreamers to follow their four-wheel fantasies.

Artistic

Artist Albert Guibara introduced a new form of "driveable sculpture" with this whimsical work called the Hippomobile. Built on a 1971 Mustang convertible, the car's body was finely sculptured in copper and brass to look like a hippopotamus. It was the "pièce de résistance" of a succession of Guibara artwork that combined fantasy with functionality and the culmination of his obsession with animal sculpture. His previous fantastical metal sculptures included dragon and alligator figures which doubled as bars; a monkey that hung from a rope in a shower; giant turtles for garden decorations; a dragonfly headboard for a bed; and an elephant-shaped desk. He also created a home aquarium in which a fish flipped out onto the wall.

Autos

Before turning his attention to doing this car, Guibara was considered a highly respected sculptor whose projects included corporate commissions such as fountains and wall pieces for office buildings. His work had been sold internationally through Alfred Dunhill of London, Ltd. and he had also done commissions for architects and private collectors.

On January 17, 1988 the Hippomobile crossed the block at the world-famous Barrett-Jackson auction in Scottsdale, Arizona. It received a high-bid of $8,500 but was not sold at that price during the sale.

Hippomobile was entered in a classic car auction.

Jungle jalopy! Although it was constructed on a 1971 Mustang, the Hippomobile was promoted as a 1980 model. Its artist-creator Albert Guibara printed his own tongue-in-cheek sales brochure for the unique vehicle.

The first page of the brochure showed a small photo of the front end of the car. It included a hippo's head. A headline read "Introducing the 1980 Hippomobile: Because it's a real jungle out there."

In the center spread of the brochure was a large three-quarter view of the vehicle and small photos depicting is features. "Genuine 100 percent hide upholstery found in the hidden elephant burial grounds," said the caption below a photo of the bucket seat interior. "Turn on the high beams and see the hippo turn on," says the caption below a second small photo showing the hippo-shaped highbeam indicator lamp.

Other interesting details promoted in the brochure are the bird-shaped outside rear view mirror, the "first real toe-truck" toe-shaped wheelcovers and a wagging tail that swings back and forth "to keep bugs off hard to reach areas."

Copy inside the brochure reads, "It's a jungle out there and it's about time there was a car company that realized it. That's why we at Hippomobile, Inc. want to welcome you to the world of the 1980 Hippomobile."

"Nothing could be hipper than wallowing in the lap of luxury in our 1980 Hippomobile. Tired of traffic jams? Have you ever seen anybody stand in the way of a Hippo? And wait until you hear the bellow of the horn — it's enough to give Tarzan a headache.

"However, we do offer a caution. DO NOT drive past a zoo ... especially during mating season (the rear suspension is tough, but may not stand up to the sex drives of a bull hippo).

"So grab a chair and a whip .. put on your pith helmet and puttees and set out on the road to adventure in your 1980 Hippomobile. You too will say, "Safari ... so goodie."

Sprayed to give them the appearance of concrete, a group of old cars are used to make an artistic statement in a sculpture called "Carhenge" that's located in Alliance, Nebraska. This 1955 Cadillac is one of the vehicles featured in the art piece.

Timeless classic. Look closely and you'll see that the wheelcover on the rear-mounted spare tire is decorated with a clock face and hands, although they are not working. This Mercedes, appearing for an auction at the Volo Antique Car Museum in Volo, Illinois, was said to have once been owned by Muhammad Ali.

"Extinct Species" is the name of artist Stephen Hooper's zebra-striped, fur-trimmed 1977 Pacer. Working under the name Hoop, he has done a series of cars that he paints and decorates with synthetic fur or miscellaneous items. "The public gives me a great reaction," he says. "Very positive."

Hoop is a Clifton, New Jersey native well known in the New York art community for his car art. This example is called "Extreme." It is based on a 1958 BMW Isetta. In addition to the multi-color cubist paint scheme, it has fur accents on the wheel openings, roof, deck and front-opening door.

"Space age primitive" is how car-artist Hoop characterizes the school of art that inspired his "Voodoo Volkswagen." The 1971 Beetle is certain to cast a spell on everyone who sees it. Note the voodoo doll mounted on top of the roof. Hoop drives the cars himself and does not sell them.

From this view, Hoop's "Voodoo Volkswagen" looks ready to sink the teeth painted on its engine lid into flesh. Hoop has had many gallery and museum shows of his conventional paintings, but says nothing gives him more pleasure than bringing the art outside and driving it down the street.

Hearse dual-gate! We're not talking about a Hurst dual-gate shifter. "Gate of heaven" is what the two monoliths providing the eerie background for this photo of "American Dreamer" say. The car, a 1941 Packard hearse decorated by Stephen Hooper (the artist called Hoop) has more of a nightmarish quality.

"American Dreamer." The other side of Hoop's 1941 Packard funeral car looks different. The artist says that people enjoy seeing his cars on the streets in New Jersey and New York City. "And I feel I give them a bright spot in their day," he adds.

Here's another art statement from Hoop. Based on a 1961 Trojan, a British-built three-wheeler, the "Recycler" features a one-of-a-kind trim package made of items you'll find in the local dump, including pop cans, snack food packages, beverage containers, old newspapers, and aluminum foil.

This 1977 Mazda has fun reflected all over it, from the helicopter and airplane crib toys on the front bumper to the slot car track on the hood. Car-artist Hoop calls it the "Flamboyant Toy." A real classy touch is the fender skirts made of synthetic fur. The roof is also decorated with plastic lawn ornaments in the shape of flowers and flamingos, as well as rows of spikes.

When Beatle John Lennon sang "Drive My Car" in 1965, he might have been talking about his 1956 Bentley. The late entertainer transformed his highbrow toy into an art statement with a custom, multi colored psychedelic paint scheme. The car was purchased by Apple Corp. in 1966 and painted by J.P. Fallon & Son. Lennon was 26 years old then. In 1968, the car was traded for a yacht. Dr. Lonnie Hammargren, of Las Vegas, Nevada, eventually bought the Bentley at an auction for $325,000. He later donated it to the ACD Museum in Auburn, Indiana.

This automotive art piece titled "Drive-In: Second Feature" was done by Robert Welch of New York City in 1982. Made of tree twigs and twine, it's a life-size rendition of a 1957 Cadillac El Dorado. It was featured in "The Road Show" exhibition at the John Michael Kohler Arts Center in Sheboygan, Wisconsin June 4 through August 13, 1989.

To end this section of WEIRD CARS we have two more photos of the "Carhenge" sculptural installation at Alliance, Nebraska as photographed in 1991 by automotive writer and historian John Lee. The cars seen in the view include a 1968 Pontiac, 1961 Chevrolet and 1960 Plymouth. How many other makes and models can you identify?

Cadillac didn't bury the tailfin until 1965, but this 1961 Cadillac included in the "Carhenge" installation symbolizes the revisions that were coming soon. The artwork represents a very weird end to the vehicles used in it. Surely none of the assembly line workers who built such cars years ago ever imagined they would "end up" (pun intended) like this.

Buses

This photo of a long, long, long old bus was included in the files of Goodyear Tire & Rubber Company. Goodyear and other tire manufacturers played a major role in the early development of the long-distance highway travel industry. The photo was taken in 1923. The bus has such a vast wheelspan that there are separate compartments for reserved seating, ladies and smokers.

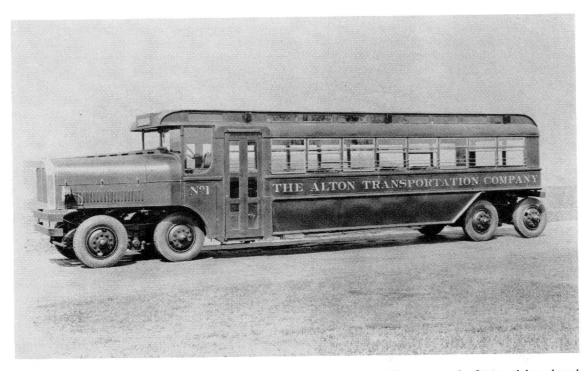

This eight-wheel bus looks like a cross between a locomotive and a street car. It was the first model produced by a company from Albany, New York. The long body, made of prefabricated aluminum panels, rode on double bogies. Each bogie was driven by an electric motor, with the current supplied by a generator driven by a Buda gasoline engine located under the conventional hood.

"It's quilllttteeeedddddd!" Kaiser's cartoon horse used to advertise on television in the 1950s. This Kaiser-Industries-built bus is also "quilted" in the middle. It's an articulated model, which means it can bend around corners. The streamlined styling and paint job add to its weird looks.

Odd vark? The "Alsacia," a 1929 sleeper coach built by the Pickwick company of Los Angeles looks a lot like a giant anteater. This so-called Nite Coach featured 13 interlocking passenger compartments on two levels, each with running water, sleeping berths and two lavatories.

"Door A, door B or door C?" this little lady might be asking. The big vehicle behind her has plenty of doors to pick from. It's a Buick sedan that was rebuilt into a motor coach by the Flxible Company of Loudonville, Ohio in 1932. The weird spelling of the word "Flexible" was done to trademark the firm's name.

Hitched to a star. Milwaukee, Wisconsin industrial designer Brooks Stevens designed two of these fifth-wheel type motor homes for the Plankinton meat-packing family. Both the trailer and the streamlined cab (with Ford V-8 power) had self-contained living quarters.

Tom and Nancy Hoefert of Chula Vista, California sent in this photo of a weird "bus" they saw in Del Mar. It is the fuselage of a DC-3 airplane mounted on a school bus chassis with a Lincoln V-8 engine installed. The sign on the side identifies it as the "Commercial Custom Coach" and advertises the insurance services, body and paint work and customizing offered by an auto body shop.

This 1967 bus was built for the county council of Leicestershire County, England for use as a mobile library. A graphic artist spent over 1,000 hours using a freehand-and-stencil technique to make the exterior look like a half-timbered cottage. Over 100 plants and flowers are painted in such accurate detail that different varieties are depicted at the stage of bloom that they would reach at a certain time, if they were all planted at the same time.

The Ultra Van was the brainchild of David Peterson, an aircraft engineer from Oakland, California. It had an aluminum monocoque body with fiberglass caps front and rear. The rear was patterned after a Spartan trailer and the front was built around a Chevrolet Step-Van windshield. In 1965, Ultra Coach moved to Hutchinson, Kansas where some 360 Ultra Vans were made. About 300 used Corvair engines. The company later became BELCO and built Ultra Vans through 1969. Some had 307 cubic-inch Chevrolet V-8s. In all, about 400 were made.

While cruising in an Ultra Van, the driver and passengers viewed the world through a three-piece panoramic windshield.

Corvair Ultra Van

By Terry V. Boyce

A collectible motor home? A motor home suitable for today's high gas prices? Both attributes in the same vehicle? Surely we're kidding! But then, if you consider the Corvair-powered Ultra Van, maybe we're not. True, it has the whimsical and nostalgic appearance of an old Greyhound bus that shrank in the rain, but the Ultra Van's pancake six power gives it double-nickel and better cruising performance.

The ready-to-roll, 4,000-pound weight, due to its unique aircraft-principle construction, allows for mileage approaching 20 to the gallon.

While parts for the van's engine and drivetrain are readily obtainable, an Ultra Van itself may be hard to come by. Less than 400 were built, mostly between 1965 and 1970. Most of the survivors belong to members of the Ultra Coach Club. This hardy group of tourists hosts frequent Ultra Van get-togethers all over the United States.

The Ultra Van began in the mind of David Peterson, a transplanted Kansas aircraft engineer who was living in Oakland, California in 1960. He liked to take his Spartan travel trailer and his boat to the beach. Life would be that much easier, it seemed, if he could motorize the travel trailer, leaving only the boat to tow. Just about that time, the Corvair arrived on the scene. Its unitized engine-drivetrain-axle was a natural for adaptation.

Peterson designed a chassis-less aluminum shell for his project, using aluminum panels for the body, which resembled a "monocoque" aircraft fuselage. Aluminum bulkheads added extra strength. Front and rear caps were formed of fiberglass. The rear section was patterned after Peterson's Spartan, while the front was created around a Chevrolet Step-Van windshield with a larger center pane of flat safety glass between the halves. Prototypes used modified and widened Corvair front axles, while the late models had Chevy II components at the front.

The Ultra Van was something of a sensation and there was a definite demand for additional copies. These appeared sporadically, with frequent changes in dimensions and specifications, until 1965. That year, a Kansas City publishing house owner made a deal with Peterson to move the tooling and himself to Hutchinson, Kansas to establish a 10,000 square-foot plant for mass producing Ultra Vans. About 360 vans were built in the Hutchinson plant, of which a little over 300 had Corvair engines. These were the most common Ultra Vans and most survivors are of this series.

The Corvair-powered, Kansas-built Ultra Vans were almost all 22 feet long. The width was 96 inches, including mirrors, while overall height was just eight feet (a six-footer could stand easily inside). The Ultra Van had a low center of gravity. Even the gas and water tanks were placed beneath the floor to keep weight close to the ground. The van's 80-inch track contributed to its stability at high speed.

Inside the Ultra Van was all of the plushness the sixties could muster. Wall-to-wall carpeting was featured. Numerous overhead storage compartments were built in. A complete kitchen, bathroom and sleeping area was included. One floor plan featured the final touch of 1965-style class by mounting a pole lamp near the left side "picture window."

Just as the Ultra Van got into something like regular production a new group of investors took over the plant. Operating under the corporate name BELCO, they built the vans in the same basic format until 1969, when Corvair production stopped. A 307 cubic-inch Chevrolet V-8 was installed in a few Ultra Vans, while a new 23-foot Tiara motor home was introduced with a 455 cubic-inch Oldsmobile Toronado power train.

At about this time, the Ultra Van operation became part of Collins Industries. They ceased all motor home production in 1972, turning to the manufacture of specialty buses, fire apparatus and other operations.

David Peterson, meanwhile, was at work on his idea of an Ultra Van for the 1970s. He planned to use a side-mounted V-8 positioned on the left-hand side of the vehicle. A venture to produce these in Sonoma, California faded in the motor home crunch arising out of the energy crisis in that era. Only two were actually built. They were far more intriguing than the original Ultra Van.

The Ultra Coach Club keeps a number of the Ultra Vans on the road. Its members live largely by a manual written by Len and Edy Ryerson. This publication has over 300 pages detailing all the things owners need to do to keep their Ultra Vans rolling down America's highways. The name Ultra Coach was used by the club to avoid negative associations with the word "van" during the 1970s. Some of the vehicles even had replacement emblems identifying them as Ultra Coaches, but they were really Ultra Vans.

Ultra Van literature stressed the definition of "ultra," saying that it meant "going beyond all others." They were referring to the van's construction and handling, of course. But, today, it seems that even in this time dimension, the Ultra Van goes beyond it contemporaries in just about every way. It's reliable, sturdy, economical and quite an attention-getter as well.

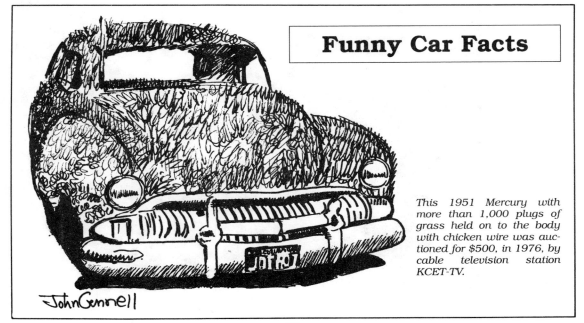

Funny Car Facts

This 1951 Mercury with more than 1,000 plugs of grass held on to the body with chicken wire was auctioned for $500, in 1976, by cable television station KCET-TV.

Custom Cars

The term "Custom Car" can apply to two different basic types of vehicles. The first is the classic, custom coach-built car turned out in the days when wealthy car buyers purchased a chassis and hired coach builders to add a distinctive body. A 1931 Franklin Airman sedan owned by Thomas C Kidd is shown above as an example.

The second type of custom is the "California Custom" or "Kustom Kar." Such terms apply to a modified production vehicle that's somewhat related to the hot rodding sport. The flamed "Shoe Box" Ford shown above represents this genre.

As you'll see, many weird cars have evolved from both of these categories.

The Custom Cloud was a customized Chevrolet Monte Carlo marketed by Custom Cloud Motors of Miami Beach, Florida. The company said it "reflects classic European styling, while maintaining the dependability of a well-built American automobile." It was sold through selected Chevrolet dealers.

The Gaylord featured a retractable hardtop that was raised and lowered by a single motor. James and Edward Gaylord commissioned famed industrial designer Brooks Stevens to style this car, which used a Chrysler 300 hemi V-8. The dual headlamps were added when it was restyled in 1956.

The body of the "Junkyard Mongrel" was hand formed from aluminum, magnesium and galvanized steel using typical aircraft construction techniques. It was created by Paul Jones, an aircraft test pilot who wanted a small, but powerful car he could park easily at crowded Elgin Air Force Base. It is registered as a 1948 Ford, apparently based on the engine serial number.

The hood, trunk lid and cockpit area were formed from a pair of 1941 Studebaker hoods placed back-to-back. The car started with a 1936 Willys chassis, a 1933 Ford axle, and 1946 Crosley brakes. Galvanized steel was used at the rear of the body to offset engine weight. Note the unusual hinged doors that drop down allowing the driver to enter.

This car has attracted lots of attention at the Antique Automobile Club of America's National Fall Meet in Hershey, Pennsylvania. The early 1950s style custom, based on a 1952 Chyrsler, features four taillamps and large exhaust ports integrated into its rear bumper. Patricia Trefz was listed as its owner.

Here are two front views of the 1952 Chrysler at Hershey. Looking like a giant-sized sports car, the unique custom has a hemi V-8 and wire wheels.

Cruising along at the "Spud City Nationals" in Stevens Point, Wisconsin is a customized 1961 Chevrolet built by Jeff and Ralph Shindell of Green Bay. The low-slung and sinister-looking hand-built El Camino-style pickup was originally a station wagon.

The famous "Tommy Lee Speedster" looks like the type of car that detectives or superheroes in early comic books were usually seen driving. This classic custom car was constructed during the 1930s by race car builder Frank Kurtis. It is based on a front-wheel-drive Cord.

This rare El Morocco was photographed at the 1991 Chevy/Vettfest in Chicago.

In 1956, a small Detroit firm started altering new Chevrolet hardtops and convertibles to look like contemporary Cadillacs. They were called El Moroccos. This continued in 1957, when this car was built. Strangely, the prices advertised for El Moroccos were the same as those for stock Chevrolets.

From the front, the 1957 El Morocco reflects its Chevrolet origins, although the bodyside trim is pure Cadillac. The name of the firm that converted the cars from full-sized Chevys to scaled-down Cadillacs was Ruben Allender Company. A total of 27 were made in 1956 and just 10 were built in 1957.

This 1930 Rolls-Royce Phantom I sports a weird combination of traditional classic lines with an early attempt at aerodynamic streamlining. Its custom coach-built body was crafted by Barker, the well-known English firm.

Chrysler built three dual cowl parade phaetons for the cities of New York, Detroit and Los Angeles in 1952. They sported a rather weird body style for the 1950s. The cars later returned to the factory and were changed to look like 1955 models, although they still have 1952 titles. All of the cars still exist. The one shown is in the Imperial Palace Auto Collection in Las Vegas.

The car corral at the Antique Automobile Club of America's 1992 Fall National Meet in Hershey, Pennsylvania turned out to be a good place to look for weird cars. One example seen at the show was this 1977 Lincoln Continental that had been converted into a pickup truck by a creative soul named Mr. G.

Mr. G's Lincoln Continental pickup truck featured a number of distinctive custom touches including four oval-shaped windows at the rear of the "cab," body graphics and pinstriping, and a special soft tonneau cover that followed the shape of the continental spare tire embossment at the rear end.

Voluminous photo files at OLD CARS WEEKLY contained this shot of a "flying saucer" car with no details about the year it was built or the model it was based on. Staff members guessed that it may have been based on a late-model Corvair fitted with 15-inch wheels and tires. It has 1955 Chevy wheelcovers.

Rear view of the first of several mystery cars in WEIRD CARS. The frame around the license plates, which seem to be of California issue, read Oraville Dodge. It looks like this "Gone Again" streamliner is all set to pick up radio signals from outer space with those big antennas.

This car doesn't seem very weird, until you realize that it's a 1961 Cadillac called the Jacqueline. Another weird thing about it is that it was named after Jacqueline Kennedy, who was considered one of the world's most beautiful women. It was handbuilt by the Italian designer Pininfarina.

Woodrow Frantz, of Nazareth, Pennsylvania built this car around 1958. It has a cut-down 1949 Ford body, upside-down 1939 Chevrolet trunk lid, and doors described as "part '49 Ford, part '36 Buick." The suspension, transmission and steering used on the Mexican red sport-custom were from a 1949 Oldsmobile.

Ken Fuertsch, of Scottsdale, Arizona sent photos of vehicles he describes as being "a little bit different." We agree. Three are 1949-1951 Ford/Mercury products. Chevy has weird taillamp treatment. Front and rear views show a mid-'50s Ford. "Daddy's Girl" pickup at bottom looks like a real "tank."

This futuristic creation is based on a 1959 Chevrolet. The "double-bubble" see-through top gives it a real George Jetson appearance. A very weird paint job finishes off the unique creation.

Another weird customizing treatment is the highly sculptured rear end on this 1959 Chevrolet El Camino pickup. Taillamps appear to be 1960 or 1961 Cadillac units.

"Way out Wheels" was the name of a set of 5 x 3-inch trading cards issued by the famous customizer George Barris in 1970. There were 36 cards in all, including this one showing the "Alvin's Acorn" television car. This hot rod had a hand-built aluminum body shaped like an acorn, plus a Mustang V-8.

The Di Dia 150 was a famous custom "dream car" designed for singer Bobby Darin. It was said to have cost $93,647.29 to build. The hand-formed aluminum body was covered with 30 coats of pearlescent paint. It had a hand-formed stainless steel tube chassis, four bucket seats and a 427 cubic-inch Ford V-8.

This custom-built car is based on a Chevrolet Corvair platform. A turbocharged Corvair six supplies power. It was constructed by Fantasy Cars of El Cajon, California and used in the movies "Condor" and "Back to the Future II." It was also seen in several television commercials and in the "Knight Rider" television series.

The Beldone has the look of a true "Kalifornia Kustom." It is a Ford-Mercury based car first built in the early- or mid-1950s. It may look familiar because it's been used in films and promotions. It was seen in the motion picture "The Patsy" starring Jerry Lewis. In 1991, the car appeared on the Hoechse Celanese calendar for the month of July. It is part of the Fantasy Cars Collection.

"The only one of its kind," says the message on back of this file photo showing a modified Chevrolet Corvette. According to the inscription, it is a factory prototype, although it is one we have not seen or heard of before. Our guess is that it's a very nicely done job of customizing an original Corvette.

Now this Corvette is definitely not a factory prototype car. It is a custom with some unusual modifications including a shelf-like rear wing, flared and extended air-scoop-style fenders and a "Venetian blind" rear window cover. Why, it even has running boards. The photo was taken in August 1987 at the Corvettes at Carlisle show in Carlisle, Pennsylvania.

Custom-bodied cars built during the "Classic Era" of the 1920s through 1940s were typically constructed on large, multi-cylinder, luxury car chassis. This one uses Dodge running gear, which is a weird choice indeed. The body obviously dates from an earlier era. This was not weird. Back then, wealthy people who liked a certain car often had a coach-builder move the body to a new chassis when the original running gear became worn or out-dated.

Randy (left) and Robert (right) Rostecki stopped by Krause Publications on their way home to Winnepeg, Canada with another weird Chrysler product that underwent a body transplant. In this case, cereal heiress Marjorie Merriweather Post had the body from her favorite prewar car installed on a postwar Chrysler Imperial chassis. The car was in the Bill Pettit Collection in West Virginia for many years, before the Rosteckis purchased it in the fall of 1984, when this photo was snapped. It has since been restored by them.

Above: This weird-looking car is part custom and part factory prototype. It was put together by race car builder Frank Kurtis on a 1942 Buick eight chassis, then used as the prototype for his first Kurtis-Kraft sports roadster of 1949 and 1950. With a few alterations, the Kurtis roadster later became the Muntz Jet.
Right: The rear of the Kurtis prototype.

Television maker Earl "Madman" Muntz (better known for stereos in later years) bought the Kurtis-Kraft business. He modified the Kurtis sports roadster, lengthening the wheelbase and making it a four-passenger car. Cadillac or Lincoln V-8s were used in most Muntz Jets. Shown is a 1952 model. Another of these cars starred in the 1992 movie "Toys" starring Robin Williams. Its weird styling was perfect for the weird plot of the film.

Double

The idea of welding the front ends of two similar cars together, with their noses facing in different directions, represents a separate category of weird cars. As we will see, people have been building cars based on this theme for many years.

There are different variations of this type of construction, too. In some cases, there are no major chassis modifications and the car can be highway-driven only in one direction, since the steering is incorporated only on the original front end. However, a few talented souls have gone even further, designing double-ended cars that have four-wheel steering. These can be operated either way.

Most double-ended cars are made from full-pillared models, with the body structures joined at the central door post. These become four-door vehicles with the doors opening from the center post. However, it is also possible to have double-enders with only a single door on each side.

Ended Cars

This double-ended 1950 Studebaker is driven in area parades by the Jaffa Temple Calliope Clown Unit. This organization is based in Altoona, Pennsylvania.

The early postwar Studebaker is an interesting selection for use as a double-ended automobile, since the all-new styling these cars introduced was very radical and different with front and rear ends that looked very similar in standard factory form.

In the early 1950s, people often made jokes about whether these cars were "coming or going" as they cruised down the street. This clown-mobile makes it even more difficult to determine which end of the car is the front, until the wheels are steered.

Two famous auto designers, Raymond Loewy and Virgil Exner, were largely responsible for the weird, but wonderful styling of the postwar Studebakers. They sold well because they were innovative, while most other cars of the era were warmed-over 1942 designs.

Is this what they mean when they talk about a Model AA? Harry J. Miller, of Sarasota, Florida constructed this double-ended Model A Ford "coupe" during the late 1950s. It was featured in POPULAR MECHANICS magazine around 1958 or 1959. By the way, Model AA is the factory designation for trucks based on the Model A, though it would certainly make a fitting description of this rig.

George Zachman, of Butler, Ohio, sent this photograph of a vehicle that he owns. He calls it his "Going Which Way?" car. It began life as a 1946 Ford and still has its original Ford drivetrain. "I have a lot of fun with this car," he advised. "The picture was taken in front of my house."

This double-ended 1955 Cadillac was spotted, in the summer of 1992, parked outside a Conoco gas station in Rawlins, Wyoming. According to a cashier there, the station owner built the car years ago. The driver's end is to the left where the radio antenna is located. It makes a great billboard for the "Always Moving Ahead" slogan of the Perkins Moving & Storage service.

Constructed by Ted Holden of Palm Beach Gardens, Florida, this vehicle is actually made from two different "badge-engineered" cars. On one end, the front of a 1981 Plymouth Champ is used. On the second end is the front of a 1981 Dodge Colt. Holden calls it his " Push You, Pull Me." This photo shows the rear end of the car, with the headlamps covered so that other drivers don't look up and get startled.

Big Foot the Clown owned this van. His real name is Bill Brown and he hails from Ramseur, North Carolina. The so-called "Two-Faced Van" had a CB, a horn that played 76 tunes, a radio and cassette player and head-lights and windshield wipers at both ends. Only one end was actually driveable. Brown was stopped by the police several times while traveling.

The "Mello Yello Limo" is a double-ended Checker co-sponsored by a local beverage distributor and a Milwau-kee, Wisconsin radio station. Note that a section has been added between the center door posts, with a small window inserted between the door glass. It's seen here at Wally Rank's Old Car Show.

Eccentric Cars

The adjective eccentric describes something that deviates from the usual or accepted path. When used as a noun, the word refers to a person who is erratic, singular, curious or off center.

In this section you will find some unusual cars that were designed or built by people who were considered eccentric. As you'll see, though they were folks who didn't "relish the commonplace," some of their uncommon ideas were way ahead of their time.

Above is a front view of the 1948 Tucker Torpedo, which has the highest profile among such vehicles, thanks to the 1988 film called "Tucker: The Man and His Dream." This Francis Ford Coppola movie traced Preston T. Tucker's true life story and focused national attention on his weird, but wonderful car.

The owner of this Edsel station wagon is very proud of the fact that it once belonged to the late General Toftoy, who was known as "Mr. Missile." It is decorated with American flags and a rocket-shaped sign honoring General Toftoy and rocket scientist Werner Von Braun.

Franklin engineers Carl Doman and Ed Marks built the 1937 Airomobile sedan for Paul M. Lewis who lived in Denver, Colorado and owned Lewis-American Airways. The streamlined three-wheeler, said to be capable of 80 miles per hour, had a four-cylinder, horizontally-opposed, air-cooled engine that produced 60 horsepower. Manufacture of a $550 production model was planned, but never realized. As happened later to Preston Tucker, Lewis was investigated by the Securities and Exchange Commission and found innocent of any stock swindles.

This eccentric car with wobbly wheels was built in 1908 by an eccentric gentleman from Washington, D.C. named Shakespeare Penn. A preacher and poet with bushy hair and white whiskers, Penn had photos taken of himself, in his car, in front of the White House.

F.C. Beamer's home-away-from-home was a ship. He was a sea captain. He ordered a weird car constructed for him. The body resembled the cabin of a ship. This allowed him to feel at "home" at home (away from boats, that is). With the seats removed, it could be converted to a sleeping berth.

Reclusive millionaire Howard Hughes was the original owner of this 1954 Chrysler New Yorker. Hughes was deathly scared of germs. He had all the windows, except the one in the driver's door, tightly sealed. He then spent $15,000 to have an air purification system installed.

The Ostentatienne Opera Sedan was the first car built by Bruce Mohs, a Madison, Wisconsin seaplane manufacturer. The only door was a hinged rear section of the roof. The car has a 119-inch wheelbase and 246-inch overall length. The 7.50 x 20-inch tires had tubes filled with nitrogen.

Bruce Mohs brought out his SafariKar in 1972. Like his earlier model, the new one was based on an International truck and had a Rolls-Royce style grille shell. However, this car had doors on the sides. They opened straight out on heavy bars, then slid horizontally along the body.

Sir Vival has Survived the Years

By R. Perry Zavitz

Survival is the name of the game and Sir Vival is the name of a safety car constructed by the Hollow Boring Company of Worcester, Massachusetts in 1959. The car's corny name and weird appearance tend to detract from the seriousness of its car safety implications.

Industrial arts teacher Walter C. Jerome, of Worcester, designed the car. As the name implies, it was based on assuring the survival of its occupants in a serious collision. Jerome hoped to convince the major automakers to purchase his safety ideas and adapt them to their own products.

The Sir Vival has two separate modules. The engine compartment and front wheels are connected to the passenger section. This means that the car can swivel in the middle. This articulated-body design seems like a very costly gimmick, in relation to the degree of safety gained through increased maneuverability.

Each module has its own extra peripheral frame for added protection in case of a collision impact from any angle. Rubber bumpers give an added degree of protection.

The Sir Vival's passenger compartment has a padded interior. Seat belts are installed inside the cabin. The rear section of the car was fashioned from a 1948 stepdown Hudson. It was designed to accommodate four passengers.

A second eye-catching feature of the Sir Vival is the driver's location. The operator of the vehicle sits up high in a turret-type affair at the front of the car's thorax. He or she is surrounded by a cylindrically-shaped windshield giving extremely broad visibility.

The car's windshield glass is canted slightly forward to enable rain and dirt to run off. If this is not sufficient, a driver-controlled rotator can actually be used to revolve the encircling windshield. In the process, it is cleaned and heated. Just below this

A 1948 Hudson was used as the basis for the rear passenger module. Turret for driver is grafted onto the fastback roof. (Jerry DiDonato photo)

Jerry DiDonato snapped this photo of the 1959 Sir Vival safety car at Bellingham Auto Sales, where the weird car "Sir-vives" today. Note the articulated, twin module body created by modifying a 1948 Hudson sedan. It is powered by a Hudson six-cylinder engine housed in the front section with the grille and conventional headlamps.

This close-up of the Sir Vival's passenger compartment shows the strange details of the rear module, such as the revolving windshield, the cyclops headlamp and the driver's turret. The car cost approximately $10,000 to build in 1959.

This view of Sir Vival shows profile of passenger cabin with driver's turret and cyclops headlamp high on front. Ahead of the cabin module is the power module with front wheels, engine and transmission.

windshield is an extra headlight, somewhat reminiscent of the 1948 Tucker's cyclops headlamp.

A Hudson in-line six-cylinder L-head engine is mounted in the forward module and hooked to a three-speed manual gear box. A flexible driveshaft is provided to transmit power to the drive wheels in the rear module. Jerome claimed to have spent $10,000 creating the car. Unfortunately, no car manufacturers lined up to order completed vehicles or buy patent rights to individual Sir Vival features.

The car still exists in the collection of Edward Moore, a collector and collector car dealer in Bellingham, Massachusetts. Moore's father sold Hudsons and was also one of few dealers for the postwar Playboy car made in Buffalo, New York. In addition to the Sir Vival, Moore has many original Hudsons and several "new-old-stock" Playboys.

Two late-1950s style fins are added to the rear and house the brake lights and parking lamps. Car is stored with many other solid antiques. (Jerry DiDonato photo)

The newcomer that received the most publicity in America's postwar auto industry was Preston T. Tucker. His 1948 Tucker Torpedo was designed by the far-thinking designer Alex Tremulis. Sharply different features of the car included aluminum, air-cooled single disc brakes; individual wheel suspension; incorporation of a "crash pad" cowl; and the use of a third front "cyclops" headlight that turned in the direction the car was steered. It was originally intended to sell for $1,845 f.o.b. at the company's Chicago factory.

The 1948 Tucker Torpedo had a long sloping fastback rear end with fin-like taillights on the fenders, just above the rear grille. The rear-mounted 334.1 cubic-inch air-cooled "helicopter" engine produced 166 horsepower. Torque convertors were used to eliminate the conventional clutch, transmission and differential. They applied direct power to the wheels from the rear engine.

Preston Tucker poses with one of his radically styled 1948 Torpedo sedans in front of his Chicago, factory.

Tucker: Birth and Death of an Innovative Automobile

By Tony Hossain

Ever since his childhood days in Detroit, Preston Tucker had lived and breathed automobiles. Like so many other youthful dreamers, he thought of bringing out his own car and beating Detroit at its own game. In almost every way, he succeeded. In the most important way, he did not.

In the mid-1940s, Tucker began assembling a staff to help him build his dream car. Tucker was well known in automotive circles, he was a good salesman and he was determined to make a revolutionary contribution to the auto industry. That he did. As the project progressed, it was apparent that Tucker would be borrowing ideas from no one. This car was to be all new and all Tucker. And with only $28 million to work with, the results were nothing less than sensational.

Alex Tremulis, a talented designer who had worked on Cords, Duesenbergs and other classics of the 1930s, had a metal prototype ready to go in 100 days. The car was sensationally styled, lower than any car then in production and featuring a much wider track. Pontiac wasn't first in this regard. But, it was the mechanics of the new car that were really intriguing.

First of all, the engine was rear-mounted and that was a dramatic departure from the tried-and-true Detroit practice. The engine itself was a 334.1 cubic-inch flat six built primarily of aluminum. It developed 166 horsepower, making the Tucker one of the fastest cars on the American road. In many ways, it was similar to the Corvair that General Motors would introduce with much fanfare some 12 years later.

Safety was an obsession with Preston Tucker and that fact was reflected in the design of the car. The body structure was extremely solid and the frame was stronger than that of any other contemporary American car. Crash padding was used on interior surfaces and the windshield was designed to pop out on impact. The integrity of the design was proven one day in 1948 when one of the first Tuckers was undergoing road testing at the Indianapolis Motor Speedway. One of the new tubeless tires blew out and the car rolled over three times at a speed in excess of 80 miles per hour. The driver walked away from the Tucker with only a bump on the leg and the car was driven away under its own power after the failed tire was replaced. The car sustained very light damage, although the windshield had popped out, just as it was designed to do.

Tuckers were brought to the courthouse in Chicago, during Preston Tucker's trial, to show that the cars worked and that charges of stock fraud were unwarranted. (Wally Wray photo)

From a standpoint of specifications, the Tucker was a real contender in 1948. It was the fastest sedan on the market, with 0-to-60 times under 11 seconds and a top speed over 100 miles per hour. And it was regularly delivering over 20 miles per gallon in Tucker's own testing. This is borne out by the owners of the 51 cars that were eventually placed in service.

Inside, the accommodations were the equal of the Cadillac and doors that opened into the roof area eased entry and exit into the unusually low (by 1948 standards) machine. Three headlamps lit the road ahead and the center-mounted one turned with the front wheels. Tucker was full of good ideas, unconventional to be sure, but good.

With articles in almost every major magazine and newspaper, the market for Tucker's new car seemed assured. There was tremendous public interest and a large number of orders were placed. Purchased from Chrysler Corporation, a plant in Chicago was all ready to begin volume production when the government pulled the plug. The Securities and Exchange Commission chose the beginning of the Tucker experiment as a good time to scrutinize the financial backbone of the fledgling automaker.

Accusations that fraudulent stock deals were being made were wildly flung about and it didn't take long for a confidence crisis to develop. Investors quickly became reluctant to put their money into a company that was considered suspect by the American government. Tucker lost his financial support and production stopped after just 51 of the advanced cars had been built.

The story does not end there. The case went to trial in 1950 and Tucker was acquitted of all charges filed by the over-zealous government agency. In the meantime, another independent automaker had bit the dust.

The real tragedy of the Tucker story is that it was a viable venture that may have been railroaded by outside forces. The car was at the leading edge of technology in 1948, and had it been given a chance, it may have had a profound impact on the way cars would have been built in the 1950s. That, of course, is just conjecture at this point.

As for Preston Tucker, he was not willing to give up the debacle. Unfortunately, he lost a bigger battle on December 26, 1956. Preston Tucker died of cancer that day.

An interest in safety was reflected in 1948's most interesting auto.

Tucker, in retrospect, was wildly ambitious. He turned those dreams into reality with a car that was technologically superior to the ones that Detroit was peddling. But, he never made peace with the all-powerful financial, governmental and business communities and, in that way, Preston Tucker did not succeed.

Of the 51 cars that were produced, a great majority of them are still in service or in museums. The car proved its worth and each surviving example retains that arrogant, independent flair that Preston Tucker admired so.

One of the cars used in the movie about Preston Tucker.

A sloping rear emphasized Preston Tucker's interest in streamlining.

Preston Tucker obtained rights to an engine made by Air-cooled Motors.

The automotive career of William B. Stout was estimable. Although the cyclecar he designed while working as a editor for MOTOR AGE was never produced, he also did the Imp cyclecar for the W.H. McIntyre Company. Later, he worked for Scripps-Booth and Packard. Then, in the mid-1930s, he created this weird-looking streamlined car called the Scarab. A limited number were made.

Bill Stout set up Stout Engineering Laboratories in Detroit, Michigan in 1932 and then built the first of his experimental Scarabs. This fully-restored 1936 model, owned by Ron Schneider of Milwaukee, Wisconsin is pictured here competing in the modern cross-country rally called The Great American Race. Schneider owns two of the Scarabs. Two more are in the Detroit Historical Museum's collection. Another is believed to be in France.

The Stout Scarab owned by Ron Schneider of Milwaukee, Wisconsin, on display during the Wally Rank Car Show.

Stout Years Ahead With Scarab

By Ken Ruddock

In the 1930s, many of America's most prestigious cars were advertised in the successful business monthly *FORTUNE*, which began at the dawn of the depression in February 1930. A typical mid-1930s issue might have full color ads for Pierce-Arrow, Packard, Lincoln, and Cadillac. But, in November 1935, an ad appeared for a rather unusual, if not outlandish automobile called the Scarab.

An illustration was done in blue and brown, by E.L. Johnston. It placed the weird-looking car on a flagstone driveway, near a country home, on a starlit evening. Beneath the car is a jeweled scarab (a gem made in the form of a large, shelled beetle) which was a symbol in ancient Egypt). The car was named for and it did, indeed, resemble a beetle. It also looked somewhat like the later Volkswagen Beetle, though the Stout Scarab was longer and wider.

Beneath the illustration was the headline, "A challenge and a prophecy." The challenge declared that a decade of aircraft and automobile research brought about this radically different, rear-engined Scarab. It called upon the big-production manufacturers to remove their conservatism and abandon traditional design. The company called it "a friendly but direct challenge" and declared that the Scarab expressed "union, functional design, individuality, and fine craftsmanship." The ad copy stated that the car was "produced by a group whose soundness of experience and engineering finesse is thoroughly established, the obvious 'rightness' of the Scarab design is its greatest challenge."

The prophecy in the ad predicted the new Scarab would set all future styles in motor cars. The manufacturer forecasted that an array of features, exclusive to the Scarab, would be adopted by all car makers within three years. "These features mark the final departure of motor car engineering from the horse-and-buggy tradition" exclaimed the ad. A long list of innovations followed, including a rear engine; unit body; elimination of running boards and fenders; thermostatically-controlled heat; grille-enclosed headlights; slanted windows; full insulation; and smooth body lines minimizing wind noise and resistance. Many of these ideas were adapted within a few short years by the major car makers.

Scarab production was limited and planned to be around 100, each priced at $5,000. Actually, only nine were built and sold. It was clearly announced in the 1935 Scarab ad that potential buyers could get a "demonstration upon invitation only." Industrial giants Willard Dow and Philip Wrigley were among the privileged few allowed to buy these custom-built cars. The Scarabs were kept up to date and were recalled every time the car's designer thought up new improvements.

The creator of the Scarab was Bill Stout, long time engineer and an automobile designer with ideas way ahead of the times. He had a special interest in aerodynamics. In fact, five years before the famous flight of the Wright Brothers in 1903, Stout made a model plane that actually flew.

Born in 1880 at Quincy, Illinois, Stout tinkered at a young age, devising and constructing toys. He earned the nickname "Jack Knife," which he later used as a pen name when he was editor of the boy's page of the *ST. PAUL DISPATCH*. He was married in 1906 and toured Europe by motorcycle on his honeymoon. A few years later, in 1910, he built a motorcycle of his own design called the "Bi-Car." It emphasized comfort and featured an automatic two-speed transmission. He also designed a motorcycle for the Schurmeir Motor Company of St. Paul, Minnesota.

In 1912, he was hired as aviation editor of the *CHICAGO TRIBUNE* and later joined the staff of two automobile magazines, *MOTOR AGE* and *AUTOMOBILE*. Between 1914 and 1916 he was chief engineer with the Scripps-Booth Motor Company of Detroit, a builder of small cars that was later absorbed by General Motors. Here he developed a lightweight cyclecar (a combination motorcycle and automobile). In 1916, he also designed a cyclecar, known as the Imp, for the McIntyre Motor Car Company. When the first Imps rolled off the assembly line, they gave Stout another challenge ... learning to drive! Up until this point, he'd never driven a car.

While at Scripps-Booth, Stout also promoted the cyclecars he designed and built, placing ads in *VANITY FAIR* and *VOGUE*. The Scripps-Booth was marketed as a second car for the well-to-do. Stout claimed he was the first to advertise automobiles without reference to mechanical specifications and first to sell the pride of owning a car.

The cyclecar craze ended abruptly by 1920, though they remained popular in Europe and Australia for many more years. McIntyre, like Scripps-Booth, never saw the early 1920s. But Stout left long before their demise. At the end of 1916, he joined Packard. There he worked once again in aviation, as a consulting engineer. His extensive research and development work on the Liberty engine lead to his appointment as Packards's chief engineer in 1917. Thousands of Liberty airplane engines left the Packard plant under Stout's supervision. After the war, he left Packard to become a technical advisor to the Aircraft Board in Washington, D.C.

He designed and built the first internally-braced cantilever airplane of veneer and wood construction, eliminating bulk and improving the efficiency of the aircraft. After this success, he founded Stout Engineering Laboratories in 1919. There he built the first American monoplane, the famous Batwing.

With his own firm, Stout began to improve on his original airplane designs. Eventually, he discovered that metal was a better material to build planes with. He contracted with the U.S. Navy to build an all-metal torpedo plane and began delivering them in 1922.

He had plans to build a fleet of commercial all-metal planes, but he needed capital to finance the project. He wrote to 100 businessmen, including Edsel Ford, Walter Chrysler and Robert Stranahan (his previous backer for the navy deal and later president of Champion Spark Plugs) asking for financial backing. Sixty of them took a gamble and helped finance an all-metal eight-passenger transport plane powered with a Liberty engine. His use of metal, the development of retractable landing gear and other Stout innovations enabled the swift development of the modern airplane. By 1926, Stout had 15 eight-passenger planes completed and the growing business was sold to Henry Ford for well over $1 million.

Next, Stout began Stout Air Services, the first regularly scheduled passenger airline service in the United States. Henry Ford was one of the backers of this new service, which carried more than 200,000 passengers in the first four years of operation without any fatal accidents. He remained vice president and general manager of the Stout Metal Airplane Company, which he had sold to Ford, supervising the construction of the famous Ford Tri-Motor plane.

In 1929, Stout sold his airline business to National Air Transport, now part of United Airlines, and left Ford's Metal Airplane Company. Stout's love was in research. He loved probing to make machines of travel more efficient and economical. Henry Ford's interest in aviation was sparked by Stout's enthusiasm and interests. Soon after he was gone, Ford lost interest in the aviation field. The last Tri-Motors were built in 1932, marking the end of Ford's venture in aircraft manufacturing.

Soon after leaving Ford, he revived the Stout Engineering Laboratories at Dearborn, Michigan, where he designed (on paper) a large 50-passenger airplane. He also had plans for a personal airplane, the Skycar, but the hard times prevented these projects from materializing.

His next project was to reshape and redesign the automobile. He thought the automobile industry was bound in tradition; locked into building boxy cars that still relied on the basic horseless carriage design. His answer was the aerodynamic Scarab, first unveiled in 1932. This Scarab was an experimental automobile, not designed to go into production. It was one of the earliest attempts to completely change the design of the automobile. This revolutionary car took aerodynamics into account to a point that styling was almost entirely forgotten. Stout raised $128,000. This was quite a sum in the early 1930s, but he did it with the slogan "Invest with me and loose your shirt." The money was used to build his first Scarab. The car was built in Dearborn at Stout Laboratories and many of the car's components came from his old friend and neighbor Henry Ford.

Ford supplied a V-8 engine, a conventional three-speed transmission, steering gear and other parts. The rest of the car, with a unitized duraluminum body and wraparound windshield, was Stout's idea. It emphasized safety, comfort, simplicity, practicality and improved performance through advanced aerodynamics. The car featured a rear engine and rear-wheel drive. Unfortunately, in 1932, America was not ready to buy a car like a Scarab and only one was built.

In the early 1930s, there were other attempts at dramatically changing the design of the automobile. Chrysler was the first to market a completely different car on a large scale. This was its 1934 Airflow. Several other pioneers experimented with different, if not so weird-looking, cars. Buckminster Fuller completed the first of three Dymaxions late in 1933. Similar to the Scarab in design, the Dymaxion was built in the former Locomobile plant in Bridgeport, Connecticut. Although the car had some

While taking part in the Great American Race several years ago, the passengers riding in Ron Schneider's 1936 Stout Scarab had to wave a sign out the rear door window advising onlookers what kind of car they were seeing.

good technology, cost overruns and negative publicity following a suspicious accident at the 1933 Chicago World's Fair caused the demise of this futuristic car in 1935.

As the Dymaxion failed, Bill Stout entered the scene with his second Scarab. This time, he had hopes of selling it on a limited basis. This new model repeated most of the features of the 1932 version, but had several differences. It featured a body of steel, instead of duraluminum, and utilized a completely different suspension system. The styling was even more dramatic. Its lines were even more aerodynamic and rounded. Another obvious feature of this 1935 version was its grille-enclosed headlights. The 1932 Scarab had used standard-type headlamps melting into the fenders, although they protruded out, similar to the famous Pierce-Arrow trumpet headlights.

The new Scarab was introduced to the public in November 1935. The main sensation of the Scarab was its rear engine, rear-wheel-drive and streamlined unit body. Stout thought the engine should be in the rear since that was where the weight was needed, especially in the winter. This also eliminated the driveshaft, enabling the car's floor to be lower and increasing the room inside it. Stout maintained this also put the center of weight below the point of support, thus letting the car bank (instead of roll) at sharp curves. Stout said that the rear engine made a lot of sense, since it would reduce bumps for passengers. The front of the Scarab was lightened for better steering and better passenger comfort. To show how well the rear-engined Scarab was able to take the bumps, Stout carried a glass of water on the dashboard, from Detroit to California, without spilling a drop. He made six cross-country trips with this Scarab, putting some 89,000 miles on it.

Another feature of the Scarab eliminated running boards which, Stout thought, were there because buggies had steps. He felt they had no purpose on the modern car. The Scarab also had vented louvers over the headlights, a chrome covering over the front luggage compartment, no-draft ventilation, electric door locks, tinted windows and coil springs at all four wheels. Each spring was bolstered by large oil cylinders which absorbed road roughness. The overall size of the car was about the same as most standard-sized 1935 cars. However, by eliminating the running boards, widening the body, stretching the wheelbase and using no long hood up front, Stout managed to provide 56 square feet of floor space inside the Scarab. This compared with an average of 28 square feet for most contemporary automobiles and allowed room for more comfort. A davenport couch and folding table were provided.

When the Scarab was displayed in 1935 and 1936, many people asked, "Which way is it going?" as they stared at the dramatically different automobile. By 1940, however, many of the car's styling innovations and gadgets were incorporated into mass-produced cars.

Despite Stout's criticism of the automobile industry and their boxy cars, he was appointed national president of the Society of Automotive Engineers in 1935. That was the same year his second, and more elaborate, Scarab was introduced.

The Scarab was not a commercial success. Only nine were built. During the 1930s, while Stout experimented with the Scarab, he earned a healthy living designing and building the Railplane. It was a streamlined, high-speed train built for Pullman service. He also developed a rear-engine lightweight bus, based on the Scarab design, for the Detroit bus system. He sold the bus development to Gar Wood Industries, which went on to build modified versions of the Stout-designed buses for quite a few years.

In 1940, Stout anticipated the era of small personal planes and developed the Skycar II. It was a small, efficient stainless steel plane billed as "the world's first motor car of the air." It was a small, aerodynamic car with wings. It was also known as a "helicar."

Stout had designed his first Skycar in 1931. It was never built. The 1940 version had four-wheel landing gear, with the wheels arranged like a car's. The front two wheels were steerable. Another of its unusual features was removable wings. They detached when the vehicle was to be used as a car. The engine and propeller were in the rear.

Stout improved on his 1940 Skycar II with redesigned versions in 1943 and 1945. He worked with Vultee Aircraft Company, in 1945, to design his fourth and final Skycar. It was more practical, and more of airplane, than the previous designs. While the idea seemed ideal for the changing times and should have worked, the Skycar never really got off the ground.

The Stout 46 or Project Y was built for Owens-Corning on Stout's own 1936 Scarab. The steel body was replaced with fiberglass and a new curved windshield was added.

At the end of 1945, Stout shelved the Skycar and began work once again on the Scarab. Working at Willow Run, Michigan with Graham-Paige (which reorganized as Kaiser-Frazer in 1946) he unveiled the ultimate Scarab. This 1946 version, dubbed the Stout 46, was based on Stout's personal 1936 Scarab. However, it was updated and redesigned along more contemporary lines. The body design indicated the 1950 trend in styling and the front end of the car looked something like the later 1951 Kaiser. The big difference with this third and last version of the Scarab was its Owens-Corning fiberglass body.

It was one of the first cars in the country to feature reinforced plastic body construction and years ahead of the Corvette and Kaiser-Darrin. It had bumpers that surrounded the entire car, wheels that were individually sprung on air cushions, and movable seats. This car also featured curved windshields and doors without handles. The entire body was molded in one large piece. There was no chassis and no axles. The air-cooled six-cylinder engine was, like previous Stout cars, placed in the rear. Stout didn't plan to market the Stout 46 and only one was built. He did, however, have plans to build a smaller version of this car to compete with GM and Ford. Unfortunately, it never materialized. The public wasn't ready for a car that had a light fiberglass body, no chassis and no axles.

In 1948, Stout retired to Phoenix, Arizona. There, he continued to experiment with revolutionary ideas until his death in 1956. Stout was a leader in aircraft development with many innovations to his name. They included the first all-metal plane. He worked in the shadows of Detroit's biggest car companies developing three different styles of cars. Each set trends in future car designs and functions. An inventor and futurist believing in change, if Stout were alive today, he would be pleased with vehicles like mini-vans. They are what he had in mind, 47 years ago, when he designed and built his dream car ... the Scarab.

Factory Show Cars

Professional model (top) and Joe Bortz (bottom) both demonstrate the proper way to stand next to a factory show car. She is beside the 1956 Pontiac Club de Mer. The well-known show car collector from Chicago is leaning on his 1954 Mercury XM-800. Weird styling brought such cars lots of attention at shows.

Years ago, Detroit designers used to visit hot rod shows to get new ideas. Now, they have started building their own hot rod show cars. The 1993 Plymouth Prowler has a hot rod look combined with all currently required passenger car equipment features. It even has an air bag.

The Prowler boasts an aluminum body and a stowaway coupe top. A 3.5-liter 24-valve overhead cam V-6 engine with special headers produces 240 horsepower. It's the first factory show car we have seen that was directly inspired by a hot rod. There were hints the car could someday be built and sold.

The 1954 General Motors XP-21 factory show car had a weird appearance and a strange engine to go with it. Both its styling and 379-horsepower gas turbine engine came from jet aircraft. This car was featured at the GM Motorama as the Firebird and was the first in a series of show cars to use that name.

The second General Motors show car in the Firebird series came in 1957. This Firebird II used an unusual metal called titanium for the first time ever in automobile construction. It was also a four-passenger vehicle. The transmission had electromagnetic controls.

A weird thing about the 1958 Firebird III was that it had no steering wheel. A single central control lever governed steering, acceleration and braking functions. It also featured remote-opening doors operated by ultrasonic sound waves. There are seven fins that serve as aerodynamic stabilizers on the car. It had a 225 horsepower whirlfire gas turbine engine.

A different type of show car was the Push-button Camper of the Future, which was built on a 1958 Ford Country Squire station wagon. The rooftop tent had a fiberglass cover that became a swing-out boat. There was a sink, refrigerator and make-up corner inside and a hidden compartment held an outboard motor for the boat.

Chrysler built a series of turbine-engined cars from 1954-1979. The 1962 Dodge Turbo Dart shown here is one of the lesser known versions. In a cross-country test completed on New Year's Eve, the Dodge Turbo Dart averaged 52 miles per hour under all types of driving conditions.

Chrysler also built a gas turbine-powered Plymouth Turbo Fury for use in a nationwide endurance run. The gas turbine engine could operate on almost any fuel that flowed through a pipe from kerosene to diesel or gasoline to furnace oil. It also had only a single spark plug.

Chrysler built 50 of the famous 1963 Turbine cars and loaned them to the public for product evaluations. Only a handful of the vehicles survive today, one at Chrysler and the remainder in private collections and museums.

Chrysler's Weird Turbine Car

By Wally Wyss

Long ago and far away ... in Berkley, Michigan to be exact ... one of my neighbors drove home a strange bolide. When he started this orange monster up, a whine would penetrate the air. It sounded like some immense turbine powering a great city. If there was any snow near the exhausts, it would turn to water under the heat. The car was one of 50 limited-production 1963 Chrysler Turbine Cars built by Carrozzeria Ghia in Torino, Italy, around Chrysler's 130-horsepower turbine engine.

In styling, the car didn't look Italian. That's because Chrysler's styling chief at the time, Elwood P. Engel, dictated how it would look. The roof line was similar to a Thunderbird of the 1960s, while the circular front headlights and basically bumperless front end had their own look. The rear end styling was pretty wild, too, with two great horizontal taillights jutting out at sharp angles and two simulated "jet exhausts."

All of the 1963 turbine cars were painted a metallic orange with orange leather interiors and a black vinyl top. Down the center of the interior was a brushed stainless or aluminum console with various switches on it. Chrysler stylists really laid on the turbine theme with turbine blade-styled wheelcovers, a turbine-style steering wheel and jet-type exhausts.

Inside the car the dashboard looked fairly ordinary, except that the tachometer read to unbelievably high numbers. The idle speed, for instance, ran from 18,000 to 22,000 rpm on the turbine. Maximum speed was 44,600 rpm. Another gauge not seen in ordinary cars was the turbine inlet temperature gauge. It let you know the temperature at the first stage turbine wheel.

My neighbor always started the car a few minutes before he was going to leave for work. His job consisted of recruiting young engineers for Chrysler; no doubt a task helped by rolling up to campuses in the jet-age turbine car! The turbine reached full operating temperature almost immediately. There was no need to warm it up, before you drove it off at full power.

The engine was controlled via an automatic shift lever labeled almost the same as an ordinary TorqueFlite transmission lever, except the word word "Idle" replaced "Neutral." The car had to have power steering and power brakes because of the excessive

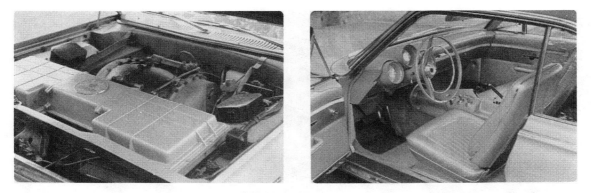

(Left photo) The turbine engine was a neat package and gave a clean appearance under the hood. The engine could operate on a multitude of different fuels including white gas, kerosene, jet fuel, diesel or a mixture of all of them. (Right photo) A handsome interior dressed the Chrysler Turbine Cars. The dashboard looked ordinary, except for a high-reading tachometer and a turbine inlet temperature gauge. Bucket type seats and a console were featured inside.

weight. I figured it must have weighed about 5,000 to 6,000 pounds. That was a lot even for the 130-horsepower turbine (equivalent to 230 horsepower in a piston engine) to pull.

One of the good things about the turbine, though it wasn't that important back in 1963, was the fact that the engine could run on just about anything. White gas, diesel oil, kerosene, JP-4 aircraft turbine fuel or any mixture of those named would do. During the energy crisis of a decade later it would have been the car to have.

Chrysler's 1963 turbine car wasn't the first in the auto industry. General Motors had built several experimental Firebird gas turbine-powered prototypes in the early 1950s, the last of which had more dorsal fins than a hammerhead shark. However, the GM prototypes were never loaned out to the public.

Chrysler took a very risky and unusual step when they ordered 50 nearly identical gas turbine cars (some had black vinyl tops and some didn't) constructed. The company then loaned them out to 203 different users in 133 cities in the 48 continental states and the District of Columbia. Poor Alaska and Hawaii were left out.

The idea behind this public evaluation was to see if ordinary American families could live with a new type of car and to see if the car worked in all types of terrain and in all kinds of weather conditions. Each loanee received the car for three months. The recipients were selected from 30,000 unsolicited letters received from car fans around the United States.

Chrysler kept a few of the cars around for promotional use and this writer remembers seeing some sort of teenage hot rod movie where the hero races someone across the country in a Chrysler Turbine Car.

Due to an obscure customs regulation, following the loan-out program, Chrysler was required to put most of the turbine cars through a buzz saw or pay a huge penalty per car to the U.S. Customs Service. A few were given to museums. Another alternative would have been to re-export them, but Chrysler officials cringed at the thought of loaning them to the wild-driving Italians!

Unfortunately, Chrysler Corporation failed to capitalize on the interest generated by the costly loan-out program and produce a production model turbine. Things went from bad to worse as the years passed. Chrysler made one bad marketing or product decision after another. By 1981, Chrysler was poised on the brink of bankruptcy.

The one bright light in the whole saga is that a much later version of Chrysler's turbine engine became the power plant for Chrysler's turbine army tank. This was a military vehicle that qualified, on paper anyway, as the ultimate full-tracked weapon ever created.

Chrysler built 50 of the famous 1963 turbine cars and loaned them to the public for product evaluations. Only a handful of the vehicles survive today, one at Chrysler and the remainder in private collections and museums.

The weirdest thing about this "El Camino" type vehicle is that it is a Pontiac. Pontiac never offered this model. In 1959, the company made one or two for use as a prototype or show car. Based on the popular "Wide-Track" Catalina, the pickup never made it to the production line.

Pontiac's "El Catalina" looked especially nice from the rear. Employees of Pontiac say one such vehicle was used as a push truck at the Pontiac, Michigan factory for years. Reports of another one being seen out west have been heard, but its existence has not been verified to date.

Every one from Wayne and Garth to car-artist Hoop knows that the Pacer is a weird car to begin with. So a Pacer pickup truck is really extra weird. American Motors Corporation built this one in 1977. How about that Mirthmobile-type flame paint job?

Just think of it as the Mirthmobile with storage room for a case of Grey Poupon. The Pacer pickup was rather short on cargo space, but made up for it in cuteness. It was made by converting a Pacer station wagon into a mini-truck.

This "chuck wagon" is a concept truck designed for exhibition at new-car shows. Based on the full-sized "Big Dooley" Chevrolet pickup, it featured a covered wagon-style canopy over the cargo box, which contained cooking equipment to feed a work crew.

The Mazda Gobi was seen on the show car circuit during 1992 and generated a great deal of excitement. The highly-stylized mini-pickup reminded some folks of a "Teenage Mutant Ninja Turtle" comic book character. It caused quite a stir among auto writers, who were told a production version was feasible.

GM design chief Harley Earl was interested in lengthening and lowering the looks of cars. The Y-Job, the first factory dream car, was based on these ideas. Franklin Q. Hershey designed the front fender extensions, which were used on 1942 GM cars. A folding cloth top stored under a metal cover. Covered headlamps and flush door handles were other highlights of the car.

Construction of the Buick Y-Job began in 1938 and ended in late 1939. It was introduced April 5, 1940. Oldsmobile stylist George Snyder was in charge of the overall design project. The car incorporated a roomy trunk that housed the automatic folding top mechanism and a 13-inch spare tire. Both the hood and trunk opened "alligator" style. The rear end design emphasized width and added to a low-slung look.

Ghost Pontiac

Best known as the "Ghost Car," this 1940 Pontiac was built with a see-through Plexiglas™ body for display at the 1939-1940 New York World's Fair and the Golden Gate International Exposition in San Francisco, California. Two cars, both slightly different, were actually constructed and one of them is known to exist today. This is the six-window Deluxe Six Touring Sedan after new 1940-style front end parts were installed in late-1939 or early 1940.

In 1939, the "Transparent Car" was put on display in section F on the lower level of the General Motors Building at the New York World's Fair. It was exhibited in front of Dean Cornwell's mural "Strength and Safety." This was the six-window Deluxe Six Touring Sedan with 1939-style front end.

The Plexiglas™ Pontiac

John A. Gunnell

The number one attraction of the 1939-1940 New York World's Fair was General Motor's "Highway and Horizons" exhibit. It was made up of several parts, the most popular being the famous Futurama presentation which offered visitors a magic flight through time and space into the world of 1960. While this part of the exhibit was concerned with the future and attempted to predict the products beyond the horizon, it is also true that the rest of GM's exhibit stressed the role of contemporary scientific research in the creation of those products. The theme "New Horizons of Industry Through Research" was used to underscore the other displays in the pavilion. These features included the "Previews of Progress" stage show, Frigidaire Division's exhibit on the mysteries of cold, an automobile salon, research laboratory demonstrations, a diesel locomotive with glass sides and the transparent, plastic-bodied Pontiacs which are the subjects of this story.

Perhaps the best way to explain GM's decision to construct transparent cars for the fair, is to repeat the words that GM president W.S. Knudsen spoke when he traveled to the fair site in a 1904 Oldsmobile to make a dedication at the pavilion's ground-breaking ceremonies. Knudsen said; "We can't begin to make progress until fear is overcome by curiosity." What could better satisfy the 1939 fair goer's curiosity than a fully transparent car that served as an open textbook of modern automotive science?

When we look closer at the cars, we see that they were a unique exercise in the use of new materials in automotive construction. However, the primary reason the cars had clear Plexiglas™ bodies had nothing to do with the use of plastic in making cars. The see-through bodies were made to allow viewers to see the structural and operating parts that reflected the corporation's latest thinking about chassis design and body construction. The Plexiglas™ exterior made it possible to see clearly the rigid interior bracing used in Fisher's new unisteel turret top bodies. The strength and safety of the new, all-steel bodies was emphasized. The fact that all-steel construction allowed increased greenhouse areas was pointed up for its contribution to increased vision and, thus, safety. As one ad copywriter slyly wrote about one car, "It shows at a glance the hidden values that are built into Pontiac cars. See what you get when you buy a Pontiac!"

Here, on a card given out at the 1940 New York World's Fair, we can see a totally different "Plexiglas™ Pontiac." This car has four-window Torpedo Sedan (GM C-body) styling and the front end parts are of 1940 design. This car was also an eight. Recent research proves this car did exist, althoug it's now thought to have been destroyed.

There were many special or all-new features that the cars demonstrated when glanced at. These included exceptionally wide doors with automatic locking mechanisms which aided safety and convenience; the first use of concealed door hinges (at some spots); floating suspension; the workings of the Fisher no-draft ventilation system, with its air control unit and forced air circulation; sealed beam headlamps; the unique safety hood lock of the alligator-type hood; improved spare tire location; improved trunk door supports; safer and more comfortable Duflex rear springs; the latest Safti-Shift gear shift controls; and the highly-touted Pontiac link-parallelogram steering system. It must be remembered, though, that the cars were built by the Fisher Body Division and displayed by them at the Fair, rather than by Pontiac Motor Division. The main idea was to show advances in body engineering typical of the entire GM line up, particularly the all-steel car body.

It is not unusual that the Fisher Body Division was called upon to create these Pontiac show cars. When I first queried former Pontiac executive John Harwood about one of the Plexiglas™ cars he answered, "Actually, it is most unlikely that Pontiac actually built the car. Rather, a show car of this kind would have been built by Fisher Body, which has always built the many show cars which Pontiac has commissioned over the years. Today, because of the high costs involved, radical show cars are rarely used. Even in the old days, a show car could easily have cost $50,000 to make."

The reputed cost of building the 1940 Pontiac Plexiglas™ cars was in excess of $25,000 according to information gathered by the former owner of one. Don Barlup of New Cumberland, Pennsylvania noted, "This must have been quite an undertaking, as my car was completely hand-built. It has to be remembered that construction of the Plexiglas™ body was accomplished during 1938 or, at the very latest early 1939, for it was reported on display at the New York World's Fair in the May 4, 1939 *NEW YORK TIMES.* The process used to create the body panels was an entirely new one. In fact, the first sheet of such material, a similar plastic laminate, had been produced by E.I. DuPont de Nemours only one year earlier in 1937.

According to Mr. William C. Wall, one of three men in charge of DuPont's 1939 World's Fair activities, work with acrylic resin materials, such as DuPont's Lucite, was an absolute new art in 1938. Only a handful of people in the country were working with such material. Earlier information given to Don Barlup had indicated that the

A photo of the "X-ray Pontiac" taken in the late 1980s or early 1990s, when it was featured at the Wally Rank Show in Milwaukee, Wisconsin. The owner of the car, since the fall of 1978, has been Frank Kleptz of Terre Haute, Indiana.

DuPont Company was responsible for producing the car's plastic shell. However, Mr. Wall said this was untrue. "There was no way that involvement by DuPont on such a project could have escaped my awareness," he explained in 1978. "I would have been consulted." Wall's information has been verified by recent research, which proves that Fisher Body Division built the plastic Pontiacs.

Wall recalled that General Motors was working with such a crystal plastic material in their styling studios in Detroit. It was used for making parts for styling mock-ups and moldings of taillight lenses. GM had as much knowledge about this type of material as anyone else at that time, Mr. Wall believed. Still, it is likely that outside firms were consulted and, more than likely, one company involved was the Rohm & Haas Company of Philadelphia, Pennsylvania. Two postcards showing one see-through car at the San Francisco Golden Gate Exposition specifically refer to the body panels as being made of Plexiglas™, which is a registered trademark of Rohm & Haas.

When I contacted Rohm & Haas, I was told they had some recollection of this project, but could find nothing in their archives to document their involvement. They did have some information and pictures of several similar projects they worked on in the mid-1960s, including a Buick Riviera show car. The two postcards from the Treasure Island show in San Francisco set off the word Plexiglas™, in one case with a capital letter and in the other with quotation marks. Other contemporary articles, photos and press releases I had gathered referred to the material as glass-like plastic, crystal plastic or transparent plastic.

Early research into construction of the cars was hampered by the fact that the one car known to survive (a Deluxe Six A-body Touring Sedan) has no serial numbers. However, an article published in an English magazine in 1940, has recently come to the attention of this car's present owner, Frank Kleptz, of Terre Haute, Indiana. It mentions the first car and proves that the second car (a Torpedo Eight C-body "slant-back" sedan) was actually constructed by the Fisher Body Division.

The old article (which was illustrated by a series of small construction photos which, unfortunately, can't be reproduced) reads as follows:

Plexiglas™ Pontiac Torpedo 8: (1) While workmen prepare this X-ray model of a 1940 Pontiac Deluxe Six Sedan for shipment, other Fisher craftsmen rush to completion a second "glass" car, a Pontiac Torpedo 8. Constructed by the body-building division of General Motors for display at the New York World's Fair and the Golden International Exposition, these cars are the only ones of their kind in the world. Exterior surfaces are of Plexiglas™, a new crystal-clear plastic, to reveal the inner construction.

The "X-ray" Car in 1978, following its restoration by Don Barlup and a Pennsylvania Pontiac dealer. This is the same six-window Deluxe Six body that was seen at the 1939 New York World's Fair. The front end parts were updated in 1940. Here it is on display at Jones Pontiac in Lancaster, Pennsylvaia.

(2) Over-heated to a temperature of 320 degrees Fahrenheit, the Plexiglas™ employed for the hood, fenders and outer body panels of the transparent Pontiac being built for exhibition purposes by the Fisher Body Division of General Motors are drawn and formed to the desired shape by dies constructed of wood, steel, and plaster. Wooden patterns, from which the original steel dies were made, are employed to insure accuracy.

(3) Fisher craftsmen scrape the surface of the molded Plexiglas™ parts by hand to remove slight imperfections resulting from the heat-treating and shaping processes. Note how the braces holding this section of the alligator-jaw hood for the Torpedo 8 show through from behind, even though the operation renders the plastic material temporarily translucent.

(4) The surfaces of the Plexiglas™ panels used in the construction of the transparent Pontiacs are gone over carefully inside and out with fine abrasives following the scraping operation. Here are two Fisher workmen hand-sanding the interior of an outer door panel.

(5) Cutting out the little trap door over the gas tank cap in the left rear fender of the transparent Pontiac Torpedo 8. Note how the hand and forearm of the Fisher workman holding the fender shows through the Plexiglas™.

(6) Assembling the Pontiac Torpedo 8 now nearing completion at one of the Fisher plants in Detroit. It is being built to show the rigid interior bracing and such features as the working mechanism of the no draft ventilation system employed in the "Unisteel" turret top Fisher bodies. Complete in every detail, save for the insulating material applied to the inner surfaces of steel outer sheathing in production models, it will be possible to drive the car out on the highway should the occasion demand.

Photos of the second car had been seen years ago, although its actual existence was never verified until Frank Kleptz got hold of this article. For a while, it was thought that the photos might have been retouched pictures of a conventional four-

This is how the "See-Through" Pontiac looked in 1974, shortly after it was removed from a storage shed where it had sat for many years. The photo was taken on the day that Walter Arnold, of Carslisle, Pennsylvania, sold the weird show car to Don Barlup, who then lived in Chambersburg, Pennsylvania.

window sedan. It seemed doubtful that a second car would have been built, considering the reported $25,000 price tag. However, it's now clear that the Torpedo Eight "ghost car" was, indeed, made.

A third type of see-through Pontiac was shown in the November 1939 issue of *NATIONAL GEOGRAPHIC* magazine and other 1939 articles. This was a 1939 six-window Deluxe Six Touring Sedan. It was depicted at the New York World's Fair against a background of an elaborate mural made by artist Dean Cornwall. The mural traced the steps in the construction of an automobile body. However, this was not a third car. It was actually the same Deluxe Six Touring Sedan that survives today. At the end of the 1939 fair season, the car was given a new Plexiglas™ nose clip with 1940 styling.

Don Barlup was a Camp Hill, Pennsylvania restaurateur when he purchased the transparent Pontiac, in October 1973, from collector Walter Arnold of Carlisle, Pennsylvania. . It seems that the car had been housed in the Smithsonian Institution during World War II. After the war, it was offered back to Pontiac and wound up being picked up by a Pennsylvania dealer who then stored it in an old shed. Walter Arnold, who had a collection of old Pontiacs, learned of the car and was able to obtain it.

When Arnold sold the car to Don Barlup, it was in a totally unrestored state. S & H Pontiac of Harrisburg, Pennsylvania restored the car for Barlup. He then kept it until 1978, using it in various displays throughout his area, including a local Halloween parade when a Jack O'Lantern was displayed inside it. In the fall of 1978, the car was sold to dealer Leo Gephart during the Dutch Wonderland collector car auction in Lancaster. It then went to Frank Kleptz' collection, where it can be seen (or seen-through) today.

This special 1958 Buick Limited convertible was specially built by General Motors for actor Dale Robertson, the star of the "Tales of Wells Fargo" television show. It cost $37,000. The car appeared in LIFE magazine and was a hit attraction at the 1958 New York Automobile Show. Today it is owned by Wally Rank, a car collector and Buick dealer in Milwaukee, Wisconsin.

Above: The interior of the "Tales of Wells Fargo" Buick features hand-tooled leather upholstery, floor-mounted rifle racks, gun holsters on the doors and cowhide-style carpeting. There are steer horns on the Buick hood emblem. The car came equipped with as many factory options and accessories as it was possible to install on a single car.

Right: Special trim inserts have show's name.

Ford's Brightest Idea:

All three stainless steel Lincolns are still around and have been fully restored.

Door graphics promote "Allegheny Metal," an early name for stainless steel.

Detailed photo shows close-up of 1936 stainless steel Ford.

The three cars have black tops and the interiors are done in dark blue leather.

the Stainless Steel Cars

Four different types of stainless steel cars were produced by Ford Motor Company over a 37-year period. This photo shows three of them: a 1936 Ford, a 1966-1967 Lincoln Continental, and a 1960 Thunderbird.

Ford's Brightest Idea:
The Stainless Steel Cars

By Gene Makrancy with Carl H. Davis

Henry Ford was an innovator. In 1925, a Ford Model TT express truck was bodied in Monel metal for use by his airline. This lightweight metal was developed by the International Nickel Company. It was an early form of what became known as "rustless steel." This metal is called stainless steel today. Ford tested it in aircraft applications, but it proved impractical for automotive production use.

In 1928, when the Ford Model A made its debut, Henry Ford used rustless steel for many of its trim and accessory parts. About three years later, he made a decision to experiment with the use of rustless steel in manufacturing auto bodies.

An ad placed by Allegheny Steel Company appeared in *TIME* magazine's Nov. 9, 1931 issue. Shown was a Model A Ford that looked normal, but wasn't. "Will next year's cars be like this?" the copy asked. "We just bought this special job with the body entirely of Allegheny Metal" (another name for stainless steel). It continued: "Our car will never need paint or polish. It will never grow dull because the body, from bumper to bumper, is Allegheny Metal. You've seen hundreds of Fords with bright parts of Allegheny Metal...headlamps, radiator shell and trim. You've seen these parts stand years of abuse with never a sign of rust. Can you picture, then, a car entirely of Allegheny Metal?"

A Quick-Facts box in the right-hand lower portion of the ad layout gave the features of Allegheny Metal as follows: (1) Resists more corrosive agents than any other alloy; (2) Can be drawn, stamped, machined, spun, cast or forged; (3) Far stronger than mild steel; (4) Will take any finish from dull to mirror; (5) Is non-magnetic; (6) Resists denting and abrasion; (7) Is readily annealed; may be welded and soldered; (8) Is produced in practically all commercial forms; and (9) Immune to chemical reactions resulting from cooking and preparation of food...does not affect flavor, color or purity of any food.

According to FoMoCo expert Gene Makrancy, the stainless steel Model A show cars used production running gear and interiors. He adds, "They had wooden floor pans." Makrancy noted the cars were built with a lot of special hand crafting and assembly work. Three were made. All were 1931 Tudor sedans outfitted with deluxe equipment features. Apparently, they carried single left-hand side mount spares. They toured to cities across the country for exhibitions. One was displayed by Ford Motor Company, the second by Allegheny Metal Company and the third by Universal Steel Company.

A total of six 1935 Ford Tudors were done in stainless steel. This is a modern photo of one of the four survivors. which is stored at Allegheny-Ludlum Steel Company's Brackenridge, Pennsylvania plant.

By 1935, Allegheny Metal Company had become the Allegheny Ludlum Steel Corporation. Stainless steel was just beginning to outgrow its adolescence. Company officials approached Ford again. This time the plan was to build six additional cars. According to a company brochure published in the 1960s, the reason for building the 1936 models was that "stainless engineers wanted to find out just how long a stainless steel car would last."

Production experts had discovered much about the properties of stainless steel since 1931. The addition of chromium to the metal made it stronger and springier than carbon steel. However, the springiness became a problem in production. They knew that it didn't stamp like mild steel. This was finally solved through the re-working of dies and the creation of new processes. Welding presented another obstacle. Ian Kiltrie, an Allegheny Ludlum official who was close to the project, told Menno Duerksen of *CARS & PARTS* magazine, "The welding equipment had to be set up to special settings to handle the stainless steel. It took a bit of experimenting." A lot of handwork and special assembly operations were necessary to build the six 1936 Ford Tudor sedans from stainless steel.

Apparently the making of all six vehicles also took longer than expected. They seem to have been made at different times. While some reports said that all of the cars left the assembly line on the same day, it is a fact that the serial numbers stamped on two of the 1936 models are 2,474 numbers apart. The "spread" between these numbers suggests that the two Fords were separated in the overall production sequence.

The stainless steel 1936s shared several distinctions from the stainless steel Model As. While the earlier cars had wooden floorboards, the newer ones had normal carbon steel floor pans, which later rusted and had to be replaced. Both the Model As and the 1936 Fords used production-type running gear and interiors. However, in the late 1960s, one of the 1936s was fitted with a non-authentic red leather interior. People who have seen this car might mistakenly believe that this was the original upholstery.

The 1936s were not identical in specifications to standard production type Fords. According to a Michigan certificate of registration for one of the cars, it weighed 3,100 pounds. That compares to 2,786 pounds for a stock model. The stainless steel cars also had the following equipment: Temperature gauge; oil gauge; ashtray; side view mirror; hot water heater; chrome wheel discs; dual windshield wipers; and locking gas caps.

Two Cleveland newspaper clippings of October 1956 and October 1962 have additional background information on the histories of the stainless steel 1936s and tell many facts. One of the 1936s, along with one of the Model As, was melted down to promote a World War II scrap metal drive. The other cars remained in the possession of Allegheny Ludlum until after the war. At least some of them had traveled over 200,000 miles by this time. One report said that two of them were painted.

In 1946, the five cars remaining in the fleet were sold for $200 each. One eventually came into the possession of an Allegheny Ludlum painter named Gerald Richards. He reconditioned it and traveled extensively, adding another 50,000 miles of use. Later, he all but abandoned the car, allowing it to be used as a play area for his kids and their friends.

Another car was sold to a man in Cleveland, Ohio. He resold it to a used car dealer in Williamsport, Pennsylvania. It was seen, about a year later, in Harrisburg. Then it dropped out of sight.

Dr. Jerome Vlk, a Chicago dentist who pioneered the use of stainless steel for straightening teeth, purchased a third car at the original disposal sale in 1946. He had it restored and used it as his daily transportation for many years. It is still in the possession of his widow and is now the only example known to positively remain in private hands.

A fourth car was sold to a Philadelphian who also had an interest in stainless steel. When he moved from the city, he took the car with him and it dropped out of sight.

The fifth car, which was kept at Allegheny Ludlum's Detroit sales office for years, was sold to F.D. Crawford of Thompson Products Company, in Cleveland. It was put into his Thompson Products Museum, which later became the Frederick D. Crawford Auto & Aviation Museum. The car is still located there today.

In 1955, Allegheny Ludlum's president, F.J. Hanley, decided to find and repurchase one of the cars. By the fall of 1956, it was under renovation. The 1956 newspaper article said, "It was badly in need of repairs and replacement of working parts," but noted that the stainless steel exterior was "in excellent condition and only needed to be cleaned."

Hanley told the press that his company's renewed desire to own one of the cars was based on a desire for public awareness. "We reach a technical audience with much of our research data and literature," he noted. "We hope to show an even greater audience the value of stainless steel with this car."

The car was the same one owned by Gerald Richards. It had first been used by employees at Allegheny Ludlum's New York sales office. Then, a company salesman bought it. He had the car only a short while, before trading it in on a newer model. Richards then obtained it, used it, and allowed it to deteriorate before selling it to his employer.

Another of the cars was repurchased by Allegheny Ludlum later. It is not quite clear whether this is the car the company had traced to Williamsport in 1956 or the one that dropped out of sight after leaving Philadelphia. In any case, the 1976 article in CARS & PARTS indicated that it was found in a private museum in Cleveland (not the Thompson Products Museum). The owner of this museum sold it back to the steelmaker. It is now kept at the company's Detroit sales office.

Rumors have placed the fifth car that survived World War II in California, Alabama and other states, especially in the South. However, extensive searching has failed to turn it up. It is not true, as reported in some articles, that some of the stainless steel cars were buried in a time capsule.

The 1936 stainless steel Ford that is stored at Allegheny Ludlum's Brackenridge, Pennsylvania factory today has traveled over 466,600 miles and has had at least four different engines. It was restored by the Greater Pittsburgh Region of the Early Ford V-8 Club of America. It has body number 7006TS27466 and serial number 183330716. There are approximately 107,000 miles on the odometer. Another car is still kept at the company's Detroit sales office. It has an earlier serial number, 18-3327242.

It was not until Monday, July 11, 1960, that another batch of stainless steel Fords rolled off an assembly line. These were built at the company's Wixom, Michigan factory. They were 1960 Thunderbirds. The Budd Company, manufacturer of regular "T-bird" bodies, was also experienced in the fabrication of stainless steel. Budd had few problems with a special assignment to fashion two special cars out of this material. Parts for both cars were produced at the tail end of the 1960 T-bird production run. This timing was based on the fact that stainless steel fabrication work is hard on conventional auto body dies because of the metal's extra strength. To prevent ruining the dies too early in the year, it was decided to stamp out the stainless steel T-birds just prior to 1961 model changeover.

Both bodies were made on regular production dies from stainless steel taken from a regular run. The Budd Company then returned them to Ford for completion. The stainless steel T-birds were powered by 300-horsepower V-8 engines. The frames and suspension parts were regular production items. Carbon steel, painted white, was used for the inner hoods, trunks and door frames. The inner wheel housings and some floor panel parts were made of galvanized steel. It was considered too difficult to stamp these parts from stainless.

After being extensively publicized and utilized for promotional purposes, the T-birds were retained by Allegheny Ludlum Steel Corporation. Both of them survive today. One is kept at the company's Brackenridge, Pennsylvania factory. The other resides at the firm's Detroit sales office. Articles stating that the second T-bird was buried in a time capsule are false. This is one of several myths about the stainless steel Fords.

Modern methods of constructing car roofs, in use by the 1960s, had caused problems when the two T-birds were made. The difficulties in roof fabrication led to the use of a different body style for the next group of stainless steel Ford products. This occurred when it was decided to make stainless steel Lincoln Continentals in 1966. Both Allegheny Ludlum and Ford Motor Company agreed that hardtop styling was out. They decided to build stainless steel four-door convertibles.

Three such cars were made at a reported cost of $30,000 each. Two of them were primarily 1966 models made for Allegheny Ludlum. While they were being hand-assembled in the shop area of the Wixom plant, Lincoln-Mercury Division decided to build a third car for its own promotional use. This last four-door ragtop was equipped mostly with 1967 style trim.

This is just one unusual fact about the stainless steel Lincolns. It came about because the cars were again assembled late in the production run. The first two convertibles were trimmed like 1966 models, but titled as 1967s. The third was updated to 1967 trim, but still had a 1966 style Continental star ahead of the front wheel opening. All three received dark blue, pleated leather interiors and black convertible tops.

Following their stint as promotional items, the Lincolns were put into storage. The Lincoln-Mercury Division neglected its car and it deteriorated and was ultimately damaged. Allegheny Ludlum later bought this vehicle, in wrecked condition, and had it repaired. Today, all three Lincolns are in excellent shape with a future as bright as their body panels.

Actually, all of the stainless steel cars that survive today at Allegheny-Ludlum are in good condition. They are sometimes displayed at old car shows. The star-shaped emblems on the doors reflect the firm's obvious pride in these historic Ford products.

After 1967, the use of stainless steel in automobiles began to decline. Now, it's usage is climbing again. Will there be other stainless steel cars in the future? Can you imagine cars like the 1985 Thunderbird 30th anniversary model, the Lincoln Mark VIII or the Taurus SHO rendered in stainless steel? Perhaps someone at Ford Motor Company or Allegheny Ludlum is thinking along the same lines.

Three stainless steel Lincoln Continental four-door convertibles were hand assembled at the end of the 1966 production run in the company's Wixom, Michigan factory. Two had mostly 1966 styling, while the third had a mixture of 1966 and 1967 trim pieces.

The 1970 Modulo was a weird-looking 37-inches high Ferrari prototype. It was created by the famous Italian designer Pininfarina. The name stood for modules. There were two modular shells, but no doors. Riders entered by sliding the upper module forward.

Exhibited at 1987 auto shows was the aerodynamic Pontiac Pursuit, a strange concept car featuring four-wheel-steering-by-wire directional control and four-wheel-drive. Its wheels were enclosed in sleeves which opened and closed as turns were made by the driver.

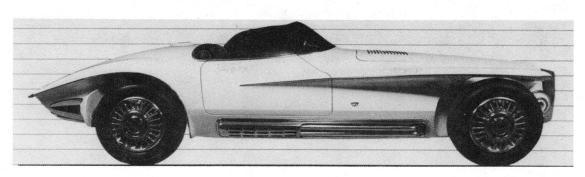

The 1964 Mercer Cobra came about because the Copper Development Association of New York City wanted to build a dramatically-styled car to highlight the beauty and functionality of copper, brass and bronze as automotive materials. Virgil Exner was asked to design the show car in 1963. It has four-wheel copper disc brakes, copper brake lines, copper instrument panel pods and a 289 cubic-inch Ford V-8 with bronze accents. The radiator shell is brass, while bronze is used for the muffler/exhaust shields, wheelcovers, headlamp trim, gas filler trim, hood vent and body rim moldings. It is on an AC Cobra chassis. The body was constructed by Sibona-Basano in Italy. Reportedly, the car cost over $100,000 to create in 1964. Dream car collector Joe Bortz purchased it from CDA in 1974. It was later sold to the Blackhawk Automobile Collection, where it's believed to be today.

The 1993 Honda EP-X show car was developed as a highly fuel-efficient commuter vehicle. It features a distinctively-styled all-aluminum monocoque body that is lightweight and aerodynamic. A unique canopy roof provides excellent visibility for both driver and passenger, who ride tandem-style. The body is specially designed to surround the occupants with a protective zone that provides protection for them in the event of an accidental impact. It is powered by a 1.0-liter VTEC-E engine that represents a new direction in personal transportation power train design.

Giant-Sized Cars

World famous customizer George Barris lengthened a 1967 Oldsmobile Toronado by 36 inches to create a limousine called the De Elegance Toronado. It had extra large doors to make getting in and out easier. Other features included a walnut entertainment console with a writing table, a television, a refreshment and cheese bar

and a stereo system. The car had a sun roof over the back seat. It was painted Silver Fine Mist and had a two-tone roof with silver vinyl at the rear and black on the chauffeur's compartment. The front-wheel-drive Toronado made a great platform for all kinds of stretched-wheelbase conversions.

Barris Kustom City was located at 10811 Riverside Drive, North Hollywood, California 91602 and Hollywood was certainly the perfect place to go cruising in the 1967 Toronado "stretch job." This may be the only one of these cars ever built.

These cars were photographed on an empty lot in Las Vegas, Nevada by Ed Dooley. He believes they were used as airport limousines and notes that they were made years before today's "super-limos" were created. According to Dooley, the vehicles were almost completely handbuilt and actually had very little Oldsmobile content.

Super-stretch Oldsmobile Toronado sports "vista" style roof, dual rear wheels, and four doors per side. A similar car with an open convertible body was used in the 1978 movie "Sgt. Pepper's Lonely Hearts Club Band."

Like many cities across the nation, Scottsdale, Arizona is doing all it can to promote "car pools." This one, in the back of a stretch limousine, was installed by Atlantis Pools, Incorporated. As you can see, it comes complete with "mermaids."

This convertible-limousine appearing at the Volo Museum Auction in Volo, Illinois during June 1992 was pro-moted as the "longest Cadillac convertible in the world." It took the driver a bit of maneuvering to park the huge ragtop inside the auction tent.

PRESIDENT LYNDON B. JOHNSON'S PERSONAL LIMOUSINE 1965 LEHMAN-PETERSON LINCOLN CONTINENTAL

Stretching over 22 feet long, this 1965 Lehman-Peterson Lincoln Continental limousine once transported Presi-dent Lyndon Baines Johnson to official functions. Its custom features included a writing console, television set, twin bars, two stereos, a dual air-conditioning system and special reading lights. Done in conservative black lacquer on the exterior, the car was upholstered in a bright blue plaid material, which Johnson is said to have liked and personally selected.

Charles and Dawnita Forell, the operators of a limousine service in Pierre, South Dakota, located this 1953 Chevrolet airport limousine in totally unrestored condition. As you can see, the car needed just about everything, including a new hood and windshield. However, the body was pretty solid.

Here is the same 1953 Chevrolet stretch limousine after restoration. This car has the body trim of a low-priced Chevrolet 150 model. There are three doors on the right-hand side of the vehicle. The left side of the body has just two doors, one far forward and the other just ahead of the rear wheel opening. The roof rack was discarded during the restoration.

This weird 1957 Chevrolet is a factory-built stretch limousine owned by John Boldt of Kaukauna, Wisconsin. It has Bel Air trim and a V-8 engine with dual exhausts. Boldt has added a sun visor, grille guard, dual mirrors and contemporary aftermarket fender skirts.

Another weird Chevrolet is this 1960 limousine, which features four passenger-side doors. It is based on the Biscayne station wagon. Sales of Chevrolet limousines was very low. Within a few years after this example was built, vans took over this market niche entirely.

Leo Weiser, president of the largest auto driving school in New York City in 1977, relaxes in his company car. The 26-foot nine-inch Cadillac stretch limousine was listed in the GUINESS BOOK of RECORDS for that year as "The Longest Car in the World."

The Longest Car in the World

The Automobile Club of America, Incorporated (ACA) welcomed New Yorkers, New Jerseyites and out-of-town visitors to the premiere viewing of its new company limousine at the Greater New York Auto Show at the New York Coliseum January 29, 1977 to February 6, 1977. ACA was the operator of America's largest driving school.

This unique vehicle was designed by company president Leo Weiser and built by A.S.C. Customcraft, Incorporated in Southgate, Michigan. Leo Weiser was celebrating his 41st year in the driver-training industry, having founded his school on December 10, 1935. The new limousine was planned as a distinctive vehicle that could promote ASC by drawing crowds to see the car's many special features.

ASC claimed that "a crew of more than 100 men and women" worked for 18 months to construct the limousine according to Weiser's plans. This probably stretches the truth as much as the workers stretched the car.

In a brochure, ACA explained the two important areas of human relations that it felt were served by the production of this car. The company's official statement said, "1) The automotive technology which has developed gradually over the past 80 years, has joined with the science of cosmetology to create enthusiasm and excitement wherever the limousine goes. 2) It has been proven beyond a doubt that imagination and inventiveness can never be computerized; the limousine was produced by all those people who helped turned Leo's original concept into an elegant, lasting reality."

The limousine had numerous special features. It was stretched to measure 26-feet nine-inches. The entire interior of the car was dyed to match the distinctive Burnt Orange Pearlescent color used to paint the body. This paint was prepared by a special formula using a unique blend of ingredients. The plump-tufted seats were upholstered in luxurious Medici velvet tapestry imported from Italy. The same material was used for the doors, ceiling, moon shades, walls, divider panels, drapes and dashboard.

The car had three doors, instead of the customary two or four. There were two doors in the chauffeur's portion of the limousine and one wide door, located on the right side, in the passenger compartment. The passenger compartment contained two L-shaped sofas, a television set (with regular and closed-circuit channels), a stereo system with six sonically-equalized speakers, two refrigerators, a bar, an intercom

103

network, a video tape-deck machine, special dome and reading lights, three telephones and an overhead air-conditioner.

A three-battery electrical system was used in the limousine, which had three separate anti-theft devices. If someone attempted to steal the car, the devices would automatically phone both the police station and squad cars prowling nearby.

The front grille featured a high-rise treatment with satin-chrome finish. A silvery Greek goddess hood ornament leaned forward, into the wind, from a special pedestal on the grille. A chrome-plated sun visor with an eight-inch brim shaded the windshield. At the rear, a real spare tire was mounted on an 18-inch stainless steel platform attached to the rear bumper. Shimmery bright metal deck straps adorned the trunk lid.

Double pinstripes decorated the body from front to rear. It had a sculptured vinyl Landau top done in decorator antique-white with accent coloring. Plush vinyl panels also trimmed the mastheads on the doors, the roof and the spare tire cover. The side windows in the passenger compartment were constructed of one-way glass allowing riders to see out, while protecting them from the gaze of people passing by. A 43-gallon fuel tank was installed.

Front and rear glass moon roofs were installed. They could be individually controlled to slide open or shut at the flick of a button. In fact, a pocket-sized remote control unit could be used to operate all of the electronic devices in the car: engine, air-conditioner, heater, defroster, and windshield wipers from up to a quarter-mile away.

Weiser used the car in television commercials for his driving school. In its edition for 1977, the GUINESS BOOK OF WORLD RECORDS published an entry about this car. According to ACA, The GUINESS BOOK OF CAR FACTS AND FEATS was also planning to list the vehicle as "The Longest Car in the World."

Leo Weiser's stretch limo was built to his order by A.S.C. Custom Craft, Incorporated of Southgate, Michigan. Because he loved autos, Weiser wanted to build a vehicle that would be distinctive enough to represent his company. The car had three doors, two for the driver's compartment and one for passengers.

Hot Rods

Ed Roth's 1963 "Beatnik Bandit" had a fully-chromed and blown 600-horsepower Olds V-8 and a "Double-duty" control stick. It was one of the weirdest hot rods ever created. (Illustration by John Gunnell)

Hot rodding started in Southern California as an outgrowth of building homemade race cars to compete in contests held on dry lakes beds. In 1948, Robert Peterson, the founder of HOT ROD MAGAZINE, put on the first rod and custom car show in the Los Angeles Armory. During the postwar years, the sport of hot rodding grew by leaps and bounds, gaining national attention.

Car enthusiast magazines of the 1950s publicized the hot rod hobby with photographic layouts of the cars. It wasn't long before professional builders opened hot rod shops in many major American towns. George Barris, "Big Daddy" Ed Roth, Dean Jeffries, Darryl Starbird and other personalities became well-known for their unusual, one-of-a-kind creations.

This section of WEIRD CARS gives a quick look at some of the stranger "classic" hot rods. If these cars turn you on, you might want to peruse the used book stores for a copy of the 1973 hardcover FAMOUS CUSTOM & SHOW CARS by George Barris and Jack Scagnetti.

By the way, the car shown in the photo above is a famous example of an early George Barris hot rod. It is based on a 1941 Ford with a much shortened wheelbase and sports a Carson top, a modified Ford flathead V-8, a LaSalle three-speed transmission and a two-speed Columbia axle. It was made in the 1960s and recently offered for sale at $30,000.

The Mr. Gasket company had this car built for promotional use. Called Chezoom, it is a very special 1957 Chevrolet built by Hot Rods By Boyd in Stanton, California. Boyd Coddington designed the smooth-looking vehicle and called it "An automotive fantasy and extremely exaggerated re-creation of the '57 Chevy that words cannot describe."

A computer-aided design system was used to create Chezoom's low-slung body. The unique "1957 Chevrolet" body was hand-fabricated, over a two-year period, by more than a dozen skilled workers. The car is powered by a 1992 Corvette LT-1 V-8 engine that produces 300 horsepower. Hot Rods By Boyd custom-designed the 17 inch Ninja wheels.

The Flintstone Flyer was built to promote the popular "adult" cartoon show that is set in the days of dinosaurs and cave dwellers. It has simulated animal skin upholstery. The car is now in the possession of Levy Ventures, a classic car dealer from Chicago, Illinois.

The Bathtub Buggy was featured at the World's Fair in Osaka, Japan. Customizer George Barris built it in the 1960s, when "kinky" hot rods were popular. The body is made of twin bath tubs painted pearlescent white. They are mounted on a hand-made frame. The Chrysler hemi V-8 has dual GMC blowers and Hilborn injectors. The interior is trimmed in grren and gold with brass accents and the wheels are gold-dipped. Eldon Toy Company made a toy version of the car.

The "Iowa Farmer" is a custom three-wheeler designed by a fellow named Chattanooga Charley and built by his brother Kenneth Whitton in 1979. That same year, a farmer from Iowa saw the trike and talked Whitton into selling it to him. That's how it got its name.

This famous Ed Roth hot rod was built in the 1960s. George Crocker of the Rear View Mirror Museum purchased it from the Bill Harrah Collection..

Ed "Big Daddy" Roth's three-wheel creation is the 1962 Rotar Air Car. It has a 104 horsepower air-cooled four-cylinder engine.

The weird thing about this hot rod is that it has a body made entirely of wood veneer. Even the wheel discs and dummy engine cover are wood.

George Barris built the Calico Surfer for Calvin Clark, the publisher of INTERNATIONAL SURFING magazine. It had a 289 cubic inch Mustang V-8.

Imports

This scene from the Walt Disney motion picture "The Love Bug" shows the hero of the film, a vintage Volkswagen Beetle, in a balancing act. Actors Buddy Hackett and Michelle Lee are performing some fancy maneuvering to keep Dean Jones (the man behind the steering wheel) on the right track. The 1965 movie was produced by Bill Walsh and directed by Robert Stevenson. Also seen in the movie was David Tomlinson. The screenplay by Walsh and Don DaGradi was based on the original story "Car-Boy-Girl" written by Gordon Buford. (Photo copyright Walt Disney Productions MCMLXVIII)

King Auto Sales, in Los Angeles, California, uses this BMW for sales promotions. The car is covered with bright green grass-cloth carpet. It seems to be the type of car that "grows" on you the more you look at it. Maybe the original owner was "Mr. Green Jeans."

Close-up photograph shows the "grass" covering the hood, fenders and bumpers of this BMW, which is used to advertise a California used car lot. This would be the perfect import for a "gay-blade" to own. In the case of an accident, you don't restore such a vehicle ... you simply reseed it.

110

A single, side-hinged door (actually the front of the car) is a weird feature of Ernest Freestone's 1957 BMW Isetta 300 Coupe. This "bubble" car was originally designed by Isowerk, of Italy, which also built the costly Iso Rivolta. BMW bought license to it in 1955. This beautifully restored example was in the Antique Automobile Club of America's Fall National Meet at Hershey, Pennsylvania.

About the only change in the 1959 BMW Isetta is the two small grilles up front. This one, owned by Howard W. Bennett, Jr. also has dual windshield wipers. The Isetta had two close-together rear wheels. However, in England it was sold as a three-wheeler to qualify it for lower tax rates on motorcycles. The mini-car cost about $1,000, but was often discounted to $800. Some Cadillac dealers gave them away as a buyer's premium. About 8,000 were imported here.

The first patrol car used by the German ADAL police force was this Model 2/10 PS Hanomag. It was nick-named the "Komiss Brot" since it resembled loaves of bread served to soldiers in the army. A 499cc water-cooled engine was mounted at the rear. It produced 10 horsepower and speeds up to 60 kilometers per hour. The car weighed 370 kilos. Only 15,775 were built.

On June 6, 1978 Milos Urban, of Czechoslovakia, left New York City's Times Square in this 1930 Tatra 12, for a cross-country tour. During the early part of the journey, the little car was hit by a tractor trailer truck and severely damaged. Urban took the car home, rebuilt it and returned to the U.S. a few years later to complete the trip.

One of the weirdest German production cars was the three-wheeler best known as the Messerschmitt. Early 1948 to 1953 versions of this car were designed and manufactured by Fritz Fend and said "Fend" on the sides of the body. It was also called the Flitzer Cabin Scooter. Since it was no longer building fighter aircraft, Messerschmitt had excess production capacity and took over manufacture of the car around 1955.

Two riders could fit into the Messerschmidt tandem-style. Frank Sennes Motor Corporation, of California distributed Messerschmitts in the United States. Mounted at the rear of the 400-pound vehicle was a single-cylinder two-stroke engine attached to a four-speed motorcycle gearbox. Top speed was 62 miles per hour.

At least 50,000 Messerschmitts were built between 1955 and 1964. The 1956 model sold for $1,073 in America. One great thing about the cars is that they could go 60-100 miles on one gallon of gasoline.

The 1948 Citröen 2CV looked like no other car in the world. It had suicide-type doors and a canvas top. Low-priced, but reliable, the 2CV was made to provide French motorists with basic transportation. MOTOR TREND called it "gawky but efficient" in 1954. Note the single headlamp and the hand-crank up front.

OLD CARS research editor Ken Buttolph tries out a Vespa for size. This mini-car was built by ACME, a French branch of the same company that built the Vespa motor scooter, which is usually associated with Italy. The cars were offered from 1957 to 1961. Even a low price of just over $1,000 couldn't make up for the lack of room inside, which held down sales of the car in America.

Somewhat strange-looking from the rear, the Tatra had a large dorsal fin on the center of the rear engine compartment lid. There were also large ducts protruding from the upper region of the lid to suck in cooling air. Like other examples of the Czechoslovakian marque, this 1951 model had unit-body construction.

The 1951 Tatra was built in Czechoslovakia. It had novel styling and engineering which struck many Americans as being weird. The body had a very streamlined appearance, enhanced by the use of rear fender skirts. The engine was mounted in the rear of the car.

By 1962, the Tatra 603 gained a hood scoop and strange air intakes mounted on top of the rear fenders. The Czech car had a top speed of 106 miles per hour and gave about 24 miles per gallon of gasoline. It was a technically advanced automobile, but seemed quite strange to most potential American buyers.

Tatraplan: Czech Rarity

By Bob Temple

The Columbia Cap Street entrance into "Beautiful Downtown" Troutdale, Oregon is also the entrance to the Crown Point Scenic Highway, a spectacular drive along the south rim of the lower Columbia River Gorge.

Whether it could be classed as scenery or not is debatable, but the first unusual sight when entering Troutdale by this route a couple of years ago was a strange little gray automobile with a prominent dorsal fin which was parked in front of a small restoration shop just to the left of the first stop sign. Needless to say, this served as an effective magnet for anyone who was interested in old or unusual cars.

The car turned out to be a 1951 Type T-600 Czechoslovakian Tatraplan with an air-cooled rear engine. Talk about rare automobiles; Tatraplans were manufactured primarily for the use of Czech officialdom. Of those exported, nearly all went to Communist Bloc nations. They weren't even sold to the Czech people. About the only way a Czech got to ride in one was to hail a taxi.

Upon stopping to check the Oregon car out, you promptly discovered that there was another identical Tatraplan inside the shop. It was undergoing the early stages of restoration. The serial numbers of the two cars were within fifty of each other. The cars belonged to Bill Meacher. The circumstances surrounding his acquisition of them are as interesting as the cars themselves.

Bill was an old car buff and a familiar swap meet vendor in the Pacific Northwest. He was especially attracted to Franklins and, so, his interests included any other rare air-cooled cars. When a friend mentioned to Bill that he had seen a strange, rear-engined, air-cooled car with a fin on it in a large parts yard at Arlington, Washington, Meacher had to go see it. I told him what I thought it might be and, since I had never actually seen one either, I went along.

I think I was expecting to see a Type 77 or the later Type 87 Tatra, but the friend had said the engine was a horizontal opposed four, instead of the V-8 which these models used. I had been intrigued by the larger Tatras ever since reading about them in the January, 1935 American *MOTOR* annual. I had forgotten about the smaller Tatraplans, but of course there hadn't been much published about them in this country.

We found the car sitting in wet weeds and grass under some tall fir trees. It looked like it had been there for a couple of years at least. The tires still held air. The car was basically straight and complete. Naturally, there was some rust, but nothing terminal.

There was nothing that couldn't be restored, except for the engine, that is. The engine was "lunched." It looked like it had been run out of oil and what was left of it had been dumped into the front end compartment. Regardless, Bill had to have the car. He made his deal with the yard owner, who agreed to deliver it to Bill's shop in Troutdale when he made his next trip to the Portland area.

About a week later the Tatraplan was unloaded at the shop. Bill's teen-age niece, who was among those frequently enlisted to help with cleanup, sanding and polishing chores on restorations, walked around the car slowly. She examined it carefully and promptly tagged it as "uncle Bill's funny automobile."

The rear of the Czech car was highly streamlined.

118

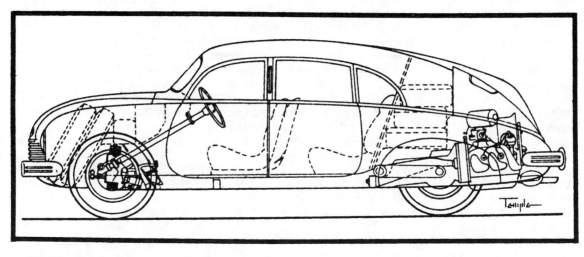

A Bob Temple phantom view of the Tatra.

What to do? Parts seemed virtually impossible to find. Maybe a Volkswagen engine would work; or possibly a Corvair motor? A crucial connecting shaft between the engine and transmission was missing. Getting another one made would be nearly impossible and very expensive.

The only sensible answer seemed to be making a complete mechanical assembly-unit switch (engine, transmission and differential) and then building up a couple of special half-axles. This would be easier than getting the special engine to transmission shaft made and fitted. It would circumvent using special adapter plates between the two.

Fabricating the transmission mounting in the Tatraplan chassis would take some doing, however, and the shifting mechanism would probably have to be re-fabricated to satisfy the new requirements.

It was about time for Bill to make his perennial tour of parts sources in preparation for the upcoming swap meets and to visit his hometown of Moose Jaw, Saskatchewan, Canada. He used to have a parts yard there and had been instrumental in establishing a museum. He still had relatives in town. More as a gag than anything else, he shot some quickie-print photos of his latest and strangest automotive acquisition and took them along to wow his hometown collector friends.

About the second day home, Bill flashed the photos on one of his friends and said, half in jest, "Here's my latest, know where I can find any parts?" The answer came back, "Yeah, there's one just like it up in Saskatoon, about a block from my folk's place, and I think it's for sale." Top that one for luck.

When Bill bought the car he got an English translated factory service manual with it. He also got enough spare parts, including the tricky-looking engine/transmission connecting shaft, to do a complete restoration on the first Tatraplan he had purchsed, if he were so inclined.

The Canadian car had been driven into its storage area, so there couldn't be too much wrong with it. Upon inspection back in Troutdale, the only thing visibly troubling it was a couple of shattered float bowls on the Solex carburetors. Since this type of carburetor is fairly common on European imports, finding undamaged ones wasn't too difficult. These were overhauled and mounted on the engine. The entire fuel system was thoroughly cleaned and primed.

The engine hand-turned freely, so oil levels were checked, a battery was installed and the engine was tested. It started, in just a few seconds, on the first attempt. It coughed, sneezed a couple of times and then ran great. No rattles, clanks, screeches or smoke. Nothing unusual either. It sounded just like a Volkswagen.

The car was comfortable and roomy enough for six adults. The seats were chair height and the faded red upholstery looked plush, although a little garish. The non-skid upholstery fabric pattern can best be described as mid-1950s chenille bedspread.

Visibility was excellent in every direction, except to the rear. The inside rearview mirror was mounted in the customary place and aligned with the rear windows. There were three consecutive sets of them. The enclosed baggage compartment was behind the rear seat, so the first window served as the front panel. The second was in the rear body panel. The third was in the engine cover and split by the fin.

The visual effect from the driver's seat was akin to peeking through a stove pipe with the damper still in it. There weren't any outside rearview mirrors on either of the cars. However, such devices would be highly recommended to any Tatraplan driver.

The instrument panel was very plain. It had a large dial speedometer on the left and matching clock on the right, the usual number of conventional switches and pull knobs, an ammeter and an idiot light for oil pressure. A center-mounted radio speaker grille and small glove box were off to the right, as I remember it. Big door pockets were used of course. The steering wheel was a 17-inch spring spoke type like mid-1930s Fords had. Turn indicators were the European illuminated arrow (Trafficator) type, which popped out of the body "B" pillars when activated. The body was unit-constructed in the manner of Lincoln-Zephyr, Chrysler Airflow, Step-Down Hudson and Volkswagen. There was a box-sectional "backbone" down the center of the floor, with box sections along the bodysides and the floor welded to the bottom. Consequently, the underside of the car was very smooth and clean. As with a Hudson, you had to step up to get out.

The Tatraplan T-600 was based on the prewar Type 97, designed by Hans Ledwinka. Hans was one of the true automotive pioneers and was an innovative thinker; to some he was radical. He was one of the early developers of features such as the backbone chassis, independent suspension, air-cooled engine, and aerodynamic body contours.

You can see a strong similarity between various features of Ledwinka's designs and those of Dr. Ferdinand Porsche. The two men were active at the same time, but were not necessarily friendly rivals. There has been an on-going controversy about who developed what for over half a century. An out-of-court 1967 settlement of $750,000, paid by Volkswagen to the Western branch of Ringhoffer-Tatra for various design infringements, was interesting.

The T-600 Tatraplan was manufactured from 1949 into 1952. Then, all automotive manufacturing by Tatra was halted for about three years in favor of production of heavy commercial vehicles. Automotive production was later resumed.

Funny Car Facts

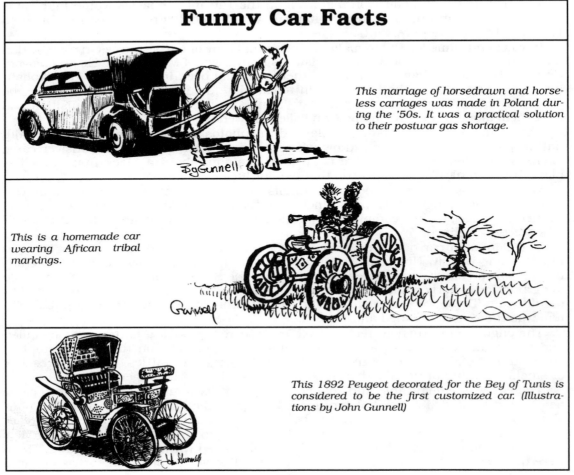

This marriage of horsedrawn and horseless carriages was made in Poland during the '50s. It was a practical solution to their postwar gas shortage.

This is a homemade car wearing African tribal markings.

This 1892 Peugeot decorated for the Bey of Tunis is considered to be the first customized car. (Illustrations by John Gunnell)

The French automaker Pahhard et Levassor was founded in 1891. In 1949, the company built this weird-look-ing car, which might have been a "dream car" or "car of the future." The name Dynamic appears on its door. However, it is quite different from the Dyna production model which retained prewar styling until the early 1950s. Then it became one of the most modern production cars in the world.

The 1949 Panhard "Dynamic" also had an unusual profile. The highly streamlined contours were predictive of the company's later models. Though the skirted front and rear fenders were not carried over on the production versions, this car's rounded lines and streamlined shape were reflected in the Dyno 110-120-130 models of the early 1950s.

The Trabant was built in East Germany. Prior to the tumbling of the Berlin Wall, it was the only type of car most average East Germans could hope to own. After reunification, the company did not survive very long. This model was called a "limousine." It had a fiberglass body and a two-stroke engine that generated enough smoke to clear a swampful of insects.

Zis is a Zis. And zat is the name of a Russian-made automobile. The initials stood for Zavod Imeni Stalin, the name of the manufacturer based in Stalingrad. Futuristic styling adapted from postwar American "dream cars" like the Buick LeSabre was used on this prototype Zis 112 hardtop. They were built in "The Factory Named for Stalin."

Jaunty Jalopies

The stars of "The Beverly Hillbillies" television show cruised into the exclusive California city in this jaunty jalopy. It was actually an antique Oldsmobile pickup truck. The popular and long-running comedy series starred Buddy Ebsen, Max Baer, Jr., Donna Douglas and Irene Ryan. Later, Hollywood customizer George Barris built a Beverly Hillbillies hot rod racing car for promotional use.

Many early motor cars look weird today. This 1895-1898 Panhard et Levassor looks like a telephone booth with wheels ... and the wheels aren't even all the same size. The manufacturer of this vehicle was organized in Paris, France during 1891. The company had started as a woodworking firm.

Karl Benz is honored as the builder of the world's first car. His firm was known as Benz & Co., Rheinische Gasmotorenfabrik, indicating that it manufactured gasoline-engined cars. The small front wheels, single acetylene headlamp, spindly wheel spokes and carriage-type top give this vehicle an unusual appearance to the modern eye.

Leon Serpollet built a car under his own name in Paris, France from 1887-1907. He was a pioneer in the steam car field. His invention of the multi-flash boiler, in 1888, contributed more than anything else to the development of steam-powered private cars. His 1899 steam road carriage has an unusual appearance representing a cross between coach building and automaking.

This 1902 Columbia Electric looks strange to modern motor vehicle lovers with its wagon-like appearance and fringed surrey top. It was produced by the Electric Vehicle Company of Hartford, Connecticut.

After 1900, Leon Serpollet took a partner in his French auto company. This 1902 Gardner-Serpollet has a boat-shaped hood, a carriage-style top and the radiator is in front of the dash. Before the concept of a "conventional" automobile evolved, a great deal of creativity was seen in such machines.

Many earlier cars, especially electric-powered taxicabs, looked similar to stage coaches. They seem weird to us today. Such vehicles are always fascinating to view and inspect at old car shows. This 1905 Columbia Electric has the driver's seat mounted high in front, with a vertical steering column.

An early attempt at streamlining gave this 1912 Darracq a weird torpedo-shaped body. It was built by A. Darracq & Co. of Suresnes, France. In 1912, this firm experimented with the Henriod four-cylinder rotary-valve engine, which proved a disaster. Another unusual feature is a radiator ahead of the dashboard.

Lucius D. Copeland made this unusual runabout by attaching a steam engine and belt-and-pulley drive system to a Star bicycle. The passenger sat up front, between the two large wheels. The small, single rear wheel was for steering. It had a weird, umbrella-like top.

This curious vehicle was constructed in 1922 by Edgar Croft of Zion City, Illinois. It featured a two-cylinder motorcycle engine with a 48-inch airplane propeller. Croft claimed 60 miles per hour and 50 miles per gallon.

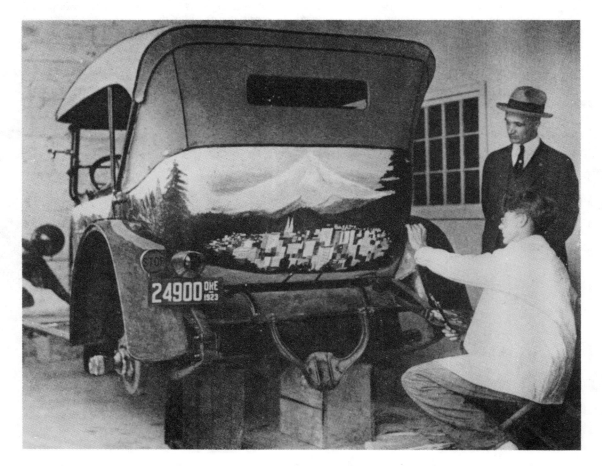

The Oregon State Motor Association planned to showcase the state's beautiful scenery with a panoramic landscape painted on the body of a vintage Pathfinder touring car. The scene depicted Mount Hood, with the city of Portland, Oregon in the foreground.

Kooky Kars

Chuck Cochoran, the owner of the Pontiac Grand Prix Museum, is also a roller coaster buff who travels the country visiting different amusement parks to ride historic coasters. Although it's purely an optical illusion, his super-imposed-photo Christmas card sets the mood for our "Kooky Kars" section. Get ready to laugh as you view the next 11 pages.

ART GROSSMANN PHOTO ©1989

NATIONAL BOWLING HALL of FAME AND MUSEUM

The Bowling Pin Car can be seen at the National Bowling Hall of Fame and Museum at 111 Stadium Plaza, St. Louis, MO 63102-1716.

The Bowling Pin Car

By Bob Loffelbein

A 1936 automobile that is as streamlined as a bowling pin because it is a bowling pin is a featured attraction of the National Bowling Hall of Fame and Museum.

This one-of-a-kind vehicle started life as an assembly line Studebaker coupe belonging to Mike Skrovon, Sr., a bowling lanes proprietor in Northfield Village, Ohio. In 1949, when he couldn't bear to part with the old "Studie," Skrovon got the idea to convert the car into a bowling pin. He enlisted Mike Skrovon, Jr. and some of his friends in the project. Hacksawing and steel chiseling off the body, they left the frame, motor, steering gear and dashboard intact. Since the boys were also setting pins on dad's lanes, this job took all summer.

In the spring, Mike Skrovon, Sr. cut his model form from two sheets of half-inch plywood. He then ordered eight 18-foot strips of steel for the actual body molding. He borrowed an old hand-cranked forge. Then, father and son heated and formed the metal to fit the plywood pattern. Five circles of steel, to hold everything together, were formed in a press at a friend's motor rebuilding shop. Then, everything was ready for welding together.

The younger Skrovon propped an old bowling pin box up as a seat and drove the stripped down Studebaker and its cargo of automotive body steel to the nearby Glenridge Machine Company. There, owner and friend Mark Negrelli spent a Sunday afternoon welding all the pieces into an entity. It took all three of them to lift the finished body over the dashboard and set it onto the frame.

Next, the car was driven back to a garage owned by Frank London, where the first work had been performed. The rest of the assembly operation was completed. Welds were double checked. The body was bolted to the frame. A wire mesh grille, seats and other comforts were added. The crowning touch, a wolf whistle, was installed.

Finally, the Don Fisher Roofing and Furnace Company was hired to cover the body with sheet metal. It took 90 pounds of body lead to cover all seams and give a smooth overall covering. Four motorcycle fenders were added when they discovered the law required fenders. The fenders were bronzed on to the car. Last, but not least, a rub-

Built in the early 1950s on a 1936 Studebaker chassis, the Bowling Pin Car is painted white with a red stripe.

ber-base paint was sprayed on. The colors corresponded to those on the real pins in Mike's Skrovon's bowling lanes.

It took five years between inception of the idea and completion. A patent was taken out on the "Pin Car" in 1958. At the same time, a sound system with a record player was added, along with a 110-power convertor for the six-volt battery. Then, the car was kept busy. It was always being readied for an event, participating in an event or being cleaned up after an event.

The car was used in parades, like the annual Bowlers' Day Parade in Cleveland. It was also popular at civic celebrations like the Bowling Proprietors of Greater Cleveland picnic. Mike, Sr. towed it to events in New York, Buffalo, Columbus and Chicago. When he retired from the bowling game in August 1962, he used the now famous car to promote his Lions Club activities, such as White Cane Publicity to benefit the blind.

At various times, Skrovon was offered $10,000 or $15,000 for the Bowling Pin Car and its patent rights. But, he loved it too much to part with it. That's why his wife or his son have never sold it. Mike Skrovon, Sr. died Sept. 14, 1973. The following year, his wife, Pauline and son, Mike, Jr. donated the car to the National Bowling Hall of Fame in St. Louis, Missouri in honor and memory of Michael A. Skrovon, Sr.

Since then, it has been used for occasional publicity projects. It became a featured attraction at the museum. In addition to serving as a traveling trademark for one of America's best loved sports, it represents a memorial to a dedicated man who did something no one else ever had.

The Bowling Pin Car can be seen at the National Bowling Hall of Fame and Museum at 111 Stadium Plaza, St. Louis, MO 63102-1716.

Santa's Rocket Sleigh is based on a 1960 Chevrolet school bus chassis. Along with Lloyd Laster's other vehicles, it was used in holiday promotions at shopping centers, mainly in the South and Southwest. A driver, two attendants, one hostess and Santa Claus formed the crew. The whereabouts of this unit are not known, although others from the fleet do survive.

Automotive historian Walter Wray photographed two of the vehicles in a salvage yard in Mazomanie, Wisconsin years ago. The front end of Santa's Rocket Ship is clearly visible. This unit has 1960 Dodge running gear. Part of Santa's Super Rocket can also be seen. Both vehicles wound up in another salvage yard in Baraboo, Wisconsin.

The people in the sleigh do not look dressed for winter. "Santa's Rocket Ship" was of a different design.

Santa's Rocket Revisited

By Dennis Schrimpf

A short article appeared in *OLD CARS* about a strange vehicle found in a salvage yard in southern Wisconsin. The vehicle appeared to be professionally built and quite unique. The only clue was the name on the side, "Santa's Super Rocket."

As is the case with many published "mystery photos," people responded. Some wanted to know the whereabouts of Santa's Super Rocket, while others expressed their opinions as to the origin of the vehicle.

Automotive historian Wally Wray, of Argyle, Wisconsin, sent us a couple snapshots he'd taken of a pair of Santa's Super Rockets in a parking lot in Mazomanie, Wisconsin. Wray didn't know what happened to the pair, but they definitely were of the same family.

The real breakthrough came when Ron Hensley of Cookeville, Tennessee sent a postcard of another Santa's Super Rocket. However, this one was called "Santa's Rocket Ship" and wasn't identical to the one in Wisconsin. On the back of the card was information about it. The card explained various specifications and features of the vehicle.

Hensley said his sons had ridden on the rocket in the early 1970s. It was part of a shopping center's Christmas season promotion. On the card was the name and address of Santa's Rocket Ship owner Lloyd Laster of Tyler, Texas. A stroke of luck provided Laster's phone number and a call was made. Mrs. Clyda Mae Laster revealed that Lloyd Laster had passed away sometime earlier. However, she had a great deal of interesting history to relate.

It seems that Lloyd Laster had built his first rocket ship in 1950. It was the "Super Rocket." A second was built in 1954 by the Hutasch Company of Jacksonville, Texas. Laster promoted the vehicles for use by department stores, shopping centers, civic groups and Chamber of Commerce organizations during the Christmas shopping season. The season usually ran from early November to Christmas Eve.

The first two rockets were built on Chevrolet school bus chassis. Two more were built in 1960, one on a Chevrolet chassis and the other on Dodge running gear. The first two were called Super Rockets, while the 1960 Chevrolet-based unit was called the "Rocket Sleigh," and the 1960 Dodge became the "Space Sleigh."

A fifth and final rocket was built in the early 1970s.

The Lasters operated in the Southern and Southwestern parts of the country. Each unit had five helpers: A driver, two attendants, a hostess and Santa Claus.

When Laster retired in 1974, Bill Griffith of Black Earth, Wisconsin purchased the rocket business. Griffith was a newspaper publisher who had seen Laster's rocket ships previously. He moved the entire operation and all five vehicles to Wisconsin.

Griffith continued the operation for another four or five years. Soon the maintenance of the vehicles caught up to Griffith. There were numerous breakdowns and delays. Ultimately, the cost of fuel and upkeep grounded "Santa's Rocket Ships" for good.

Griffith had two of the sleighs parked in Mazomanie, Wisconsin for a time. These were the ones Wally Wray photographed. Two of the vehicles (both of those built in 1960) were sold to Bill Siros' auto thrill show in Texas. One ended up in the salvage yard in southern Wisconsin. The fate of the two that Griffith parked in Mazomanie is stranger yet.

Wray mentioned in his letter that someone thought they had seen a rocket at a surplus and salvage operation called Delaney's, near Baraboo, Wisconsin. A call to Delaney's verified that the two rockets Wray had photographed in Mazomanie were later sold to Delaney's. They in turn sold both units to a party from Oke, Alaska. Whether or not the rockets ever made it to Alaska will have to be another story.

Original photos of Santa's Rocket Sleigh were used for publicity.

Did He Trade in His Sleigh?

By Dennis Schrimpf

Who would believe such a thing existed, but there it was, "big as life and twice as ugly," as the old saying goes.

Ken Buttolph and I were on our way to some show or other when I asked him if he'd mind stopping at this salvage yard in southern Wisconsin. Of course Kenny protested loudly and vehemently, but since I was driving, we stopped.

"What to our wondering eyes should appear but a miniature sleigh and eight tiny reindeer." Well, it certainly wasn't a "tiny sleigh" that appeared to our wondering eyes. Instead, it was a giant six-wheeled apparition dubbed "Santa's Super Rocket."

Upon looking it over, it became apparent that this was not the work of amateurs. It looked professionally done and with some forethought. The owner of the salvage yard wasn't sure of its history, but thought it had been used by a large shopping center during the Christmas season. The interior suggests that the seats were meant for little people. As with the exterior, the interior was finished and complete.

The vehicle is built on a school bus chassis. Vandals have broken all the windows and it will be just a matter of time before it becomes unclaimable. I wonder if the elves could put it back together?

A California used car agency transformed this Cadillac into a boat to "fish" for new customers. They hoped this would send customers "sailing" into the dealership. Apparently, they have some cars to sell to anyone who can "float" a loan. We don't know what a "Smog Sail" is, but it costs $19.

The sales manager yells "all hands on deck" when a prospect shows up. In the rear is a swiveling seat for the salesmen to use when they are "reeling in" customers. Maybe they sell only Marlins and Barracudas here.

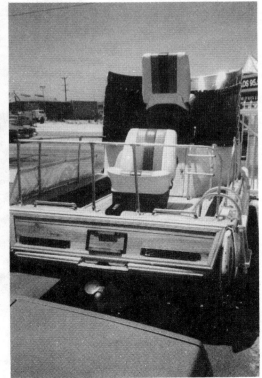

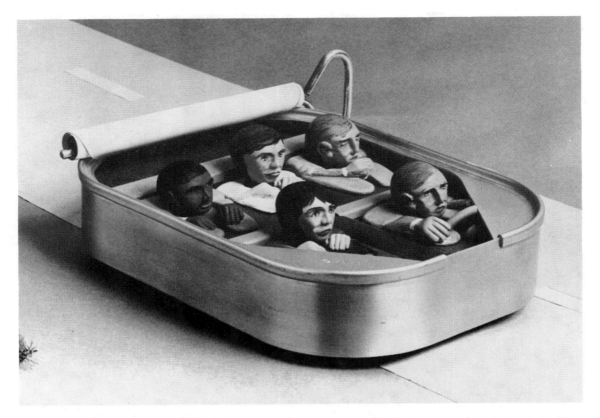

This is a photograph that appeared in a Chrysler press kit several years ago, rather than a real vehicle. However, we thought it looks like a prototype for the convertible shown below.

A customized Dodge Colt wagon was converted into a convertible by Fantasy Cars of El Cajon, California. Company owner Bob Butts hopes that this car might someday find stardom in a surfing movie or similar film. As you can see, the ragtop "woodie" features six-passenger seating.

This car was built to promote one of Mattel Toy Company's products called the Land Shark or Land Monster. It is based on an electric-powered golf cart. The mouth goes up and down as the car moves. It is part of the Fantasy Cars Collection in El Cajon, California.

The Shark Car is powered by a Volkswagen engine. It steers with an electric actuator. Fantasy Cars is trying to find a sponsor for the vehicle. "Sea World" would be perfect, says owner Bob Butts. "Or a tuna manufacturer or fresh fish company."

One of Louie Mattar's major achievements was designing this on-the-go tire changing system.

Louie Mattar's Non-Stop Cadillac

By Bob Loeffelbein

In 1954, Louie Mattar and two companions created a weird car to set the world's "non-stop" distance driving record. The car's wheels never once stopped turning on a trip from Anchorage, Alaska to Mexico City, Mexico.

The Mattar Car started out life as a 1947 Cadillac four-door sedan. From the outside, it still looks pretty much as it did then. But, when you open a door or lift the hood you may get a jolt. Scarcely a square inch of the entire body remains the same as installed at the factory. Everything, including a kitchen sink, was packed into or under the car.

The Cadillac weighed over 8,500 pounds by the time Mattar completed it in the early 1950s. The front and rear springs were reinforced with angle iron to compensate for holes cut in the body to install new systems and equipment. The extra poundage did not include the 50 gallons of water it carried.

Drinking water was piped to a faucet located in the right rear wheelwell, usually hidden by a flap in the fender. Shower water, hot or cold, was pumped under pressure to the right front fender. The radio antenna was converted into a shower head. It could be used from the running board. Water was also needed for the hookah, or water pipe, installed beside the driver's right knee. "Much better for you than cigars or cigarettes," Louie, a native of Lebanon, once guaranteed. "Besides, there is never a danger of accidental fire."

Water was used in the back seat, where a sink was built in. There was also a console containing a medicine cabinet, fluorescent lights, a mirror, an electric stove and a refrigerator with a 20-cubic inch deep-freezer. There was a combination washing machine and bidet which both used water, too.

"We can add a clothes wringer to that when we have to rinse out a few things along the way," Louie said. "There is even a small ironing board built atop the old-fashioned mid-seat armrest, so we don't have to wear wrinkled shorts on a trip." The entire housekeeping console could be pushed back into the trunk space at bed time. Then the double seat flopped over into a double bed. Positioned overhead was a seven-inch television set. "A true Johnny Carson fan never misses his show," Louie explained back in the pre-Jay Leno era.

138

One could hardly miss the built-in bar with its six spigots of refreshments ranging from bourbon-and-soda to hot water for tea. A record-playing turntable with a mobile telephone unit and an intercom was originally used (later replaced by a tape recorder). A loud speaker system could also be hooked up to use for demonstrations at fairs and auto shows. Over 50 trophies attested to the drawing power and ingenuity of the Mattar Car.

These innovations were unique, but the big changes were under the hood. Since tire and engine failures were major considerations, Louie engineered hydraulically-retractable running boards. The hood had port holes in it so that, when raised, it didn't impair the driver's view. An automatic air pump kept steady pressure in the tires, even if one picked up a nail. When a tire needed changing, the driver pushed a button and retractable running boards slid out from under the car and locked into place. A small work platform slid manually onto pipe fittings attached to the frame. The driver flipped another switch and a small airplane wheel lowered to the roadway, allowing the regular wheel to be raised for repairs.

Each wheel could be operated independently of the others. Each tire had its own pressure regulator. Air (up to 200 psi) could be bled through the axles into tires that gained or lost pressure. The car's oil could be automatically changed in the motor. Water could also be added to the radiator or used to cool the brake drums, while the car was rolling. All this was accomplished automatically via a mass of controls and gauges on the double dashboard. A co-pilot was needed to monitor the gauges and handle emergencies or maintenance.

Power to run all systems was supplied by four circuits producing 110 volts AC from specially-built batteries carrying 1500 amps. They were equivalent to 15 standard batteries. The generator put out 90 amps with the engine idling. The complex systems in Mattar's way-out rigs required a caboose full of tools, parts, spare tires and batteries to remain operative. He developed a special utility trailer to hold an extra 230 gallons of gas, 15 gallons of oil and 30 gallons of water, along food supplies. The trailer, of course, had its own system of wheel jacks for tire changing. Much of the liquid supply was handled effortlessly, through a siphoning system from trailer to auto.

Mattar, a modest man, attended no engineering school and claimed no special genius. "Like all auto innovation," he grinned, "mine involved a lot of trial and error." The Cadillac, sold for $6,000 originally, cost him about $75,000 to modify. It was not sponsored by any automotive product suppliers. Mattar was later offered more than enough to recoup his expenses, with usurious interest, if he would sell the car. However, the Mattar Special was never sold. "What price can you put on a part of your life?" he asked.

Louie's brainstorm idea to set a long-distance non-stop driving record didn't jell all at once. It just sort of grew until the ache was there to do it. As the Cadillac became well known, Louie started driving it to hospitals and orphanages with lighted Christmas trees on a turntable in the back seat. This led to the need for the tape player and loud speaker system. "As we took longer and longer trips, like on a St. Jude's Hospital fund-raising trip to Chicago with my fellow Lebanese Danny Thomas, I added the automatic water and oil change systems and the cooling system and drilled the axles so the tires could be kept pressurized equally. It wasn't until, all this had been done, that we started seriously talking about a cross-continent trip."

All the bugs were worked out after some 11,000 miles of test driving. Then a record non-stop run, from San Diego to New York and back, commenced. That trip was made September 20-27, 1952. The 6,320-mile journey took Louie Mattar, Joe Mitchell (an aircraft worker) and gas station owner Ernie Bashera a week to complete, with each driving five-hour shifts. They refueled "on the fly" from tank trucks at airfields in Kansas, Missouri, New Jersey and Nebraska.

This trip was the ideal shake-down cruise for Louie's spectacular non-stopper from Alaska to Mexico City. This 7,482-mile journey took eight days at an average speed of 45 miles per hour. It was completed August 18, 1954 at a personal cost of $12,000. Mattar spent a year just programming border clearances, police escorts and refueling stops. The relief crew this time included son Leroy and auto salesman Joe Henderson.

Harlow Forme's weird touring car looks like a fairly normal antique auto at first glance. However, those thick, angular fenders hint at its strange construction. The car is called the "Cement Special" because its body is made of cement.

The E. K. Cargill Company of 2120 Forsyth Road in Macon, Georgia built this race car in the early 1950s. The body was fashioned from aluminum jettison tanks obtained from war surplus suppliers. A two-cylinder engine was used to propel the torpedo-shaped speedster. The manufacturer claimed a top speed of 50 miles per hour and said it could go 75 miles on a gallon of gasoline. The chassis, differential and transmission came from a British Austin. The wheels, tires and seats were from an airplane. The area behind the seat was used for storage. Mass-production of these cars was envisioned.

Little Cars

Little cars look weirdest with big folks stuffed inside. On top, two ladies ride in a 1955 Eshelman Adult Sport Car. On bottom, a 1949 car that Robert Ferreira of Danville, California built in a high school shop. A 1.5 horsepower water-pump engine drove the vehicle made from a surplus airplane wing tank.

This young fellow looks as happy as a "bug in a rug." And why not, since he's driving a Cootie. The miniature car was one of several models built by Custer Specialty Car Company of Dayton, Ohio. It was designed for kids and was sold by the famous F.A.O. Schwartz Company toy store in New York City.

In addition to the Cootie, L. Luzern Custer's company produced the Coupe shown above, a miniature train called the Cabbie, a three-wheeled chair called the Electric Chair and a truck called the Carrier. Electric power was used. It's possible just one Custer Coupe was made, though the firm lasted to the 1960s.

This is one "Electric Chair" that seems like it could be fun to test out. This vehicle was offered by Custer Specialty Car Company in 1930. Luzern Custer was an invalid and understood the need for such a machine. The electric-powered automotive wheelchair was the company's best-selling model for many years.

C.L. Wright built this kid-sized car at the Hysham Garage and Machine Shop, in Hysham, Montana, during 1931. It used a battery for power and weighed 300 pounds.

Weirdly enough, this little car started life as a big one. Don Manning, of Lockport, Illinois cut down an Overland Model 91 to get parts for his Manning Midget. The 1,275-pound mini-car was made in 1932. It was promoted as sufficiently roomy for two persons, but looks like a tight squeeze for one.

For the Lilliputs

Ken Morehouse was a big promoter, but his car wasn't that "big" of a deal. It was called the "Little Mystery." His honeymoon turned into a publicity tour with Morehouse driving and his bride posing as a "hood ornament." The Detroit, Michigan native spent $9,000 on the car, which did nearly 100 miles per hour.

Thanks to the twin headlamps mounted high alongside its radiator, the 1914 Dudley Bug bears a resemblance to a praying mantis. The car was built in Menominee, Michigan by H.F. Tideman. He advertised that "everybody is bugs" about his car. This is thought to be the only surviving example.

Harry A. Williams built his miniature car in two Ohio cities, Cleveland and Akron, around 1906. It was advertised as "radically different in many respects from all others." This wasn't an economy car, as the body was made of solid cast iron and was quite heavy. The small roadster was priced at $760.

The Cricket was as cute as a bug. This cyclecar was manufactured in Detroit, Michigan in 1913 and 1914 by adding an extension to a motorcycle frame. It had an 84-inch wheelbase, weighed 500 pounds and used a nine-horsepower engine.

This car caught our eye at the Antique Automobile Club of America's 1992 Fall National Meet in Hershey, Pennsylvania. It looks like a large car that someone washed in hot water and shrunk. Actually, the Stellite is an English economy car built from 1913 to 1919 by a subsidiary of Wolseley Motors Limited.

The weirdest thing about the Weber is that it was a miniature replica of the full-sized Moon, a car built in St. Louis, Missouri. Built by a firm that made timesaving shop equipment, the Weber was used as an advertising gimmick. Later, the car was sold and seen as an attraction at the Indiana state fair.

This juvenile car of 1910 had just about everything full-sized cars featured. It was built by the Swanson brothers, of Stromsburg, Nebraska with a one-half-horsepower engine. Features included battery ignition, a splash lubrication system, cone clutch and sliding gear transmission. It weighed 156 pounds.

147

With a car like the 1925 Batchelor, you were likely to stay single for a long time. It didn't have much room to carry around the wife and kids. J.H. Batchelor, of Savannah, Georgia, built it from parts obtained in a salvage yard. He once took a trip to Miami Beach, Florida in his vehicle.

This was certainly a "smart" looking little roadster. And why shouldn't it be? After all, the metal used to make its gas tank came from the roof of a building at M.I.T. Earnest Johnson, of Beverly, Massachusetts, also used a 1908 Simplex hood, a Chevrolet 490 transmission and Pierce control parts in his car.

In 1921, MOTOR AGE reported that the Breese was "the smallest car in the world." It had a 20-horsepower Harley-Davidson engine and weighed 400 pounds. Lieutenant Robert P. Breese, a member of the United States Aviation Service, used many airplane parts to build the vehicle, which was possibly assembled in Europe. It was ultimately purchased by a French duke who liked to drive midget-sized automobiles. The wheels and tires used on the car were standard aviation parts.

James Martin, of Long Island, New York, designed the Martin-Dart mini-car in 1928. His concept was to sell motorists a car and a garage for $200. It was advertised as "the smallest car for practical purposes ever made." With a 60-inch wheelbase and 600 pounds weight, top speed was about 50 miles per hour.

James Vernon Martin's return to automaking in 1948 led to construction of a weird three-wheeler that had a single tire at the rear. The car had an aluminum body and unusual magnetic-automatic transmission. In 1950, it was given a new wood-paneled body like those used for "woody" station wagons and was called a Statio-nette.

The Chester L. Eshelman Company of Baltimore, Maryland manufactured two types of small, weird cars. Shown is the 72-inch-long Sportabout, which was made from 1953 to 1958. Automotive historian George H. Dammann says it had "the world's all-time ugliest grille." From 1955-1960, the firm made what looked like a child's car, except that it could hold one adult and do 70 miles per hour!

The passengers rode in tandem in this 1914 Economy Car cyclecar, which was built by a Providence, Rhode Island company. This kind of vehicle was an early attempt at providing Americans with economical personal transportation. The manufacturer announced an overly-optimistic plan to sell 6,000 of these.

"My car is no weird car," wrote Jeff Gibson. "It is, by all standards, a normal car, except for one thing: it is the smallest street-legal car according to the 1993 GUINNESS BOOK OF WORLD RECORDS." Documentation actually says that it was the smallest car registered in the United States in 1945.

Short Car Was a Long Time in the Making

The size of an automobile has no relationship to the time that it takes to build it. The 88-3/4-inch long Arbet owned by Jeff Gibson proves this. It was constructed by a machinist named Arliss who started the project in 1945 and did not complete the job until 1956.

Arliss hand-manufactured over 5,000 parts for the little vehicle, which has just about all of the features that a conventional vehicle boasts. There are windshield wipers and washers, multi-beam headlamps, a horn, a cigarette lighter and a heater.

The car, a hardtop-convertible, measures seven feet four inches from end-to-end. It has a 40-inch-wide body and stands 38-1/2 inches tall. Nevertheless, it is designed to carry two people and provide them with full weather protection and reliable transportation.

A two-cylinder gasoline engine is used to power the Arbet. Arliss combined his name with that of his wife Beth to name the car. Over the years, he traveled more than 14,000 miles in it. During one of those trips, 14 years ago, he left it in a parking lot where Jeff Gibson spotted the vehicle.

"I thought it was a French car," Gibson said. "A few days later, I saw it again and pulled in behind it to follow the guy home." Several years ago, Gibson looked up Arliss once more. This time, he offered to buy the car. After taking possession, he started the process to get the vehicle entered in the *GUINNESS BOOK OF WORLD RECORDS*.

Gibson, a native of Lynden, Washington, enjoys entering the car in shows these days. He enjoys driving it and laughs about his experiences, especially the time that a lady saw the car in a parking lot and asked him not to leave until she got her husband to come and look at the Arbet.

Someone sliced a chunk out of the middle of this 1951 Plymouth to turn it into a short-wheelbase model. They also added a rumbleseat. It was seen at the Barrett-Jackson collector car auction in Scottsdale, Arizona in January, 1989. The stubby ragtop drew a high-bid of $15,500 but did not sell.

If you take a few letters out of the word Impala you get Imp, which makes a great name for this vehicle. After all, it's the result of whittling a couple of feet off of a 1966 Chevrolet Impala station wagon. The "Imp Estate Wagon" was seen at the Iola Old Car Show in Iola, Wisconsin.

Media Mobiles

BONNIE AND CLYDE AMT MOVIE CAR

Above: In 1967, Warren Beatty and Faye Dunaway played Clyde Barrow and Bonnie Parker in the motion picture "Bonnie & Clyde." George Barris built the Hollywood movie car used in the film. Bullet holes were actually shot into it with a 45-caliber Thompson submachine gun.

Right: Gary Primm, owner of Whiskey Pete's, poses with real Bonnie & Clyde Ford.

Whiskey Pete's Casino, at the southern end of the Nevada state line, bought the real Bonnie & Clyde death car for $250,000. It can be seen there today.

Hal Roach Studios used a specially-built car on a 1936 Buick chassis in the film "Topper." Anthony Gerrity designed it and Bohman and Schwartz, of Pasadena, California made the custom body. Hidden controls were used when the ghost was supposed to be driving it in the movie. The car was later sold to the Gilmore Oil Company for promotions at races. Mobil Oil absorbed Gilmore and added a matching trailer with an electronics and public address system. The car received a face-lifting in 1948. In 1952, Christian Bohman, Jr. restyled it again and had the body remounted on a Chrysler chassis.

Leo Carillo, who played Pancho in the "Cisco Kid" westerns on early television, ordered this convertible from Chrysler in 1948. In addition to the steer's head mounted on the front, it had steer hide on the seats and door panels. It wound up in Bill Harrah's auto museum and was later purchased by the Imperial Palace Auto Collection of Las Vegas, Nevada. It is there today.

Concordia II was a car made for the movie "Black Moon Rising." The futuristic-looking car has a rather sinister appearance. It is finished in black and red. It looks very fast with its racing-type wheels and huge rear deck lid spoiler.

Farrah Fawcett helped George Barris pick the design, color and upholstery for her "Foxy Corvette." The interior is done in suede and flowered materials with hand-sewn "Fs" and hearts that were the Fawcett's trademarks. Two cars were built for the AMT model company. Features included a television and four-channel telephone. Passport Transport of St. Louis, Missouri transported the car, along with (left to right in background) the Green Hornet car, Liberace's 1954 Cadillac convertible, Zsa Zsa Gabor's "Gold Rolls" and the television Batmobile. All of these cars were created by George Barris.

George Barris and Dean Jeffries joined forces to turn a 1965 Chrysler Imperial into a super-hero car that Van Williams and Bruce Lee could drive on the "Green Hornet" television series. Three of these cars were eventually constructed. Special crime-fighting equipment included road tack sweepers, bullet-proof body parts, radar and rocket launchers under the rear bumper.

George Barris, the well-known customizer from North Hollywood, California, poses inside his Barris Kustom Industries shop with some of his best-known creations. Barris built his first balsa wood car models when he was eight years old and made his first two customs while attending high school.

GREEN HORNET CAR

Actors Van Williams (left) and Bruce Lee (right) starred in the Green Hornet television series, slong with a customized 1965 Chrysler Imperial.

Green Hornet's Black Beauty
Has Changed Over the Years

"Stepping through a secret panel in the rear of the closet in his bedroom, Britt Reid and Kato went along a narrow passageway built within the walls of the apartment itself. The passageway led to an adjoining building that fronted on a dark side street. Though supposedly abandoned, this building served as the hiding place for the sleek, super-powered 'Black Beauty,' the streamlined car of the Green Hornet.

"Britt Reid pushed a button. The great car roared to life. A section of the wall lifted automatically, then closed as the gleaming Black Beauty sped into the darkness."

So began Fran Striker's weekly radio drama about the super hero named Green Hornet. In the radio programs, first heard over Detroit's WXYZ on January 31, 1936, listeners heard about the crime-fighter's car Black Beauty. It was referred to as "the powerful" machine and described as a car good for "easily overtaking" the crooks. But other than such vague references, radio listeners had to form their own mental picture of the car driven by Green Hornet.

It wouldn't be until the 13th episode of the Green Hornet serial films (adapted from Striker's radio drama by Universal Studios in 1939) that anybody got a glimpse at Black Beauty. Comic books of the day depicted the sleek, super-powered car as a GM-like two-door sedan. However, after three years of dreaming by radio listeners, the Black Beauty film car turned out to be a virtually stock Lincoln Zephyr.

In his sinister-looking Zephyr, newspaper publisher Britt Reid (a.k.a. Green Hornet) fought those who "sought to destroy our America." He flew down the alleys and back streets of *THE DAILY SENTINEL*'s circulation area and occasionally made forays through the winding roads of the countryside.

A quarter of a century later, came a revival of interest in the Green Hornet. In addition to tapes of the radio program and replays of the 1939-1940 Saturday matinee films, fans were purchasing new issues of Green Hornet comic books like never before. Then, in September 1966, came the half-hour "Green Hornet" television crime drama starring Van Williams and Bruce Lee. It lasted only until the following July, but it did bring about the creation of a new Black Beauty.

This time, the crime-fighter's car was based on the 1965 Chrysler Imperial. Actually, three of the cars were made. Hollywood customizers Dean Jefferies and George Barris were co-builders of the cars, according to Barris Kustoms. Press reports of the day reputed that $50,000 had been spent on the project.

No matter how much lead two customizers added to the already beefy Imperials, the new Black Beauty's 440 cubic inch V-8 should have given them a horsepower edge over most crooks. Like the Black Beauty from the radio series, it also had some other special crime-stopper features.

George W. Trendle, who more or less "produced" the Green Hornet radio show, made sure that the original Black Beauty, described over the airwaves, was capable of such period bootlegger tricks as raising a smokes screen and dropping tacks on the road. The "boob tube" version boasted even more. It had a television camera that could see four miles ahead; an exhaust apparatus which spread ice over the road to foil pursuers; and brushes that lowered behind the rear wheels to sweep away tracks scattered in the road.

The Imperial bodies were customized in steel. Then, Roy Johnson applied 25 coats of black and green "pearl-essence" lacquer to them. Finally, Bob Bond pin striped the cars. They featured Western mag-style wheels, Firestone tires and a Kraco stereo system.

After the television series' abbreviated run, the cars were no longer needed. Barris Kustoms kept one at its North Hollywood, California facility. A second car went to the Chicago Antique Historical Car Museum owned by J.J. Borne. The third car was purchased by an enthusiast. When last heard of, it was being driven on a daily basis. Later, the car kept by Barris was entered in a 1983 Rick Cole auction and J.J. Borne's Black Beauty was sold when he liquidated his museum with a Kruse International auction.

(Editor's note: Portions of this story that describe early Green Hornet cars and information are based on an article by Micheal Scott that appears in *BEST OF OLD CARS* number five.)

Five Batmobiles were built by Barris. The original was based on the 1955 Ford Futura factory show car. The replicas featured Ford chassis and big-block Ford V-8s with Holman & Moody race car-type modifications. The front of the Batmobile was designed to look like the face of a bat. At the rear end there were triple rocket tubes and twin parachutes. Later, Barris built several Batcycles, including a special one for Batgirl.

The Batmobiles still attract crowds at many car show appearances each year, such as this one at St. Ignace, Michigan. The cars have a special paint finish that looks like the skin of a bat and red-orange trim. A radio-controlled AHI/Remco toy replica of the Batmobile is a popular collector's item today.

When the real Futura was converted into the Batmobile, the front was restyled to look like the face of a bat. It gained a hood scoop with a nose-like appearance extending down into the frontal area. "Eyes" were added on either side. They extended out to form "ears" equipped with dual 450-watt laser beams. Hidden behind the ears were functional headlamps to use for normal street driving. The grille cavity was reformed to resemble the mouth of a bat.

At the rear, dual 84-inch bat fins with "bulletproof" steel coverings afforded additional protection for Batman and Robin. Operable red reflector taillamps were mounted in the rear of the bat fins.

Four six-inch flared eyebrows and bulletproof wheel wells were designed as tire protectors. Ten inch wide Western wheels fitted with Mickey Thompson tires gave the Batmobile the handling power needed to fight villains in Gotham City. Triple rocket tubes shooting colored-fire rockets were located in the rear upper panel. The special electrical system used on the Batmobile was an Autolite devised 12-volt setup with a convertor for 110-volt AC outlets.

The Batmobile's famous 360-degree turns were made possible by pulling an emergency "Bat Door" lever. It released and billowed two bat-impression Deist parachutes attached to a 25-foot cord. At the rear, a turbine exhaust finned air-cooling tube was mounted on a v-cavity rear grille section with parachutes installed on each side.

As for the copycat Batmobiles that were used as film doubles and for promotional purposes, these were constructed on Ford chassis. The cars all had big-block Holman & Moody racing engines, B & M hydro-stick automatic transmissions, Western wheels, Firestone tires and Kraco stereo systems. They had fiberglass bodies like the original.

A number of miniature replicas of the Batmobile were licensed to be made by toy and model companies. For instance, AHI/Remco produced a radio-controlled toy which was engineered by Les Turbowitz. All of these are highly collectible toys today. In addition, the full-sized Batmobiles remain a big-draw attraction at many major rod and custom car events.

(Above) The '55 Futura show car. (Top right) The "Caped Crusaders" get ready to go to work. (Center right) Batmobiles are still big crowd-pullers on the rod and custom circuit. (Lower right) This is Fantasy Cars' replica of the original Futura.

Dick Van Dyke, Sally Ann Howes and Lionel Jeffries starred in the 1968 United Artists motion picture "Chitty Chitty Bang Bang," based on the book written by Ian Fleming, who also wrote the James Bond spy-adventure series. The imaginary flying car featured in the movie was named after a series of real racing cars.

Count Louis Zborowski built three airplane-engined "Chitty-Bang-Bang" racing cars. Two are seen in small photos flanking the "Chitty-chitty-bang-bang" movie car. The original "Chitty" of 1921 (left) had a Mercedes body and 23-liter Maybach engine. The second car (above) also had a Mercedes body.

"Ecto I" was the name of the modified 1959 Cadillac "professional vehicle" that co-starred in the 1984 motion picture "Ghostbusters" with Bill Murray, Dan Aykroyd and Sigourney Weaver. As seen in the movie, the car was rigged out with a load of heavy-duty equipment designed to aid the heros' paranormal investigations. Another star of the Ivan Reitman directed film was the Sta-Puff Marshmallow Man. A successful "Ghostbusters II" sequel was done in 1989.

Inventor Doc Brown (Christopher Lloyd) explains the workings of his Delorean time machine to a fascinated Marty McFly (Michael J. Fox) in Steven Spielberg's 1985 movie "Back to the Future." The Delorean played an important role in the film's exciting climax in which Marty races the clock to return to his own era. "Back to the Future Part II" was a 1989 sequel.

This is the actual 1907 Thomas Flyer that won the 170-day-long New York-to-Paris Race of 1908. Harrah's Automobile Collection purchased the car from the late Henry Austin Clark, Jr. It was in worn condition and had to be completely restored to the form seen in this photo. Harrah's shops did a great job on it.

Amazingly, the 1907 Thomas Flyer is still race-ready. Here we see it out for a test spin, prior to its Goodyear tire company-sponsored entry in the 1986 Great American Race. It was one of over 100 cars that traversed the country from Disneyland, California to New York City in the annual antique car rally.

After four years of dreaming about it, Blake Edwards began work on "The Great Race" in late 1965. The film was based loosely on the 1908 New York-to-Paris Race and cost $8,000,000 to make. Over $100,000 was spent on building custom-made vehicles. Here we see Tony Curtis (Leslie Galant III) and Natalie Wood in the "Leslie Special" with Jack Lemmon (Professor Fate) acting as a hood ornament. According to Bob Butts of Fantasy Cars, the body of this vehicle is made of PVC plastic, while the fenders, running boards and other parts are metal. Four such cars were built right in the studio shops. One was later used in the movie "Good Guys and Bad Guys" with Robert Mitchum and George Kennedy.

Front view of Hannibal 8 from the Great Race movie shows the spike in the center of the front of the car. This is actually the "elevator" car without the motor. On the left is Professor Fate's rocket-powered rail runner, which is actually powered by a Corvair engine in the base of the machine.

The "Leslie Special" and "Hannibal 8" from the Warner Brothers film, "The Great Race."

Hollywood's Great Race
Fun, But Not Authentic

By S.P. House

Like almost everything else it attempts to do, Hollywood's recreation of automobile history tended to become confused, if not actually silly. When director Blake Edwards (the creator of the motion picture "10") decided to do a film about the New York to Paris race of 1908, facts were thrown to the winds.

Not that a few people didn't try to retain a few threads of historic accuracy. The cars used in the race by Jack Lemmon (Professor Fate, the villain) and Tony Curtis (The Great Leslie) have become two of the most famous film vehicles in the annuals of motion pictures.

Rescued from the scrap heap in the late 1960s by James F. Brucker, founder of Movie World Cars of the Stars (a now defunct automobile museum) the cars continue to survive as examples of the film colony's daffy creations.

The "Leslie Special," is a loose artist's conception of the Thomas Flyer that actually won the race. The original resides in Harrah's Automobile Collection in Reno, Nevada. It's film counterpart is vastly different as one might expect.

A front view of the "Hannibal Eight" shows the spike, the small brass cannon and the firm front suspension.

A modern Ford V-8 was originally slipped under the hood and four-wheel hydraulic brakes installed for safety and convenience. The chassis was a modified truck frame and the body, designed by the Warner Brothers' art department, was a combination of many cars, probably none of which was a Thomas. The long, sweeping fenders looked vaguely like those of an American Underslung. The hood looked like that of a late 1920s Mercedes Benz SSK. To pinpoint the body design, take your pick of several styles by custom car builders.

A carbide generator was mounted on the running board, but it was not functional. The massive brass headlamps were, of course, electric. Wheels for the car, (again for safety) were cast metal. They reportedly cost the studio more than $500 each. A num-

Fake twin radiators dominate rear view of the "Hannibal Eight." Spare tires are made of sponge rubber.

One of the "Leslie Specials" is in the Fantasy Cars collection in El Cajon, California. Another is owned by collector Bill Goodwin of Franfurt, Indiana.

171

A Corvair engine powers the functional "Hannibal Eight."

ber of spares were made, just in case. These wheels handled the torque from the modern power plant quite well. They were not prone to snapping into splinters during stunts as wooden spokes might have done. However, they still retained the look of an antique automobile part.

One of the studio drivers who did a few of the stunts in the Leslie reported it capable of reaching speeds in excess of 90 miles per hour, but when the body and fenders started to shake, he stopped the car and refused to drive that fast any longer.

Warner Brothers made two Leslie Specials so that, in case of an accident, production wouldn't be stopped. It was also possible to do long shots of the auto with a second unit crew (none of the stars were in the car), while the more close up dramatic scenes, with the actors, could be shot elsewhere.

Professor Fate's car was of even more interesting and less authentic design. Again there were two vehicles. However, they were not identical.

One was built on an angle iron frame and had six wheels. The car's body was made of fiberglass. It had a ray gun device pointing straight ahead as another whimsical Hollywood touch. The four rear wheels were wooden and actually came from an antique car. The front wheels were wire spoke types from an unknown source. Fake carbide lights were fitted to the front fenders. There was a spotlight on the hood of the vehicle, which was called the "Hannibal Eight."

The "Leslie Special's" wheels are of modern construction. The headlamps look authentic to the era of the original race.

172

The second Hannibal Eight had a scissors type mechanism. This allowed the body to be raised almost six-feet into the air. The mechanism was a masterpiece of workmanship and was good for a few laughs in the film.

A number of actual antique cars also appeared briefly in "The Great Race." The majority of these were from movie car rental firms and were in a sorry state of condition.

For all of the failings inherent in "The Great Race" it was jolly good fun to watch. The film continues to entertain millions of people each year when it appears occasionally on television. It might make the original participants in the New York to Paris Race turn over in their graves, but as entertainment it is a winner.

Styling of the film hero's car somewhat resembles a Mercedes-Benz SSK roadster of the mid-1930s.

Hannibal cockpit: Big crank at left powers the windshield wiper. Below it is the cannon control lever. Switches are for lights, cannon firing, and smoke-screen generator.

Leslie driver's view. Lever on steering column is auto trans. gear selector. Dashboard is not "cluttered." Canteen hangs on windshield post.

Detail of Hannibal's front wheel structure. Frame "horns" are box-sectioned quarter-inch steel. The Hannibal has a "firm" ride, no "roll."

Hannibal's rear tandem wheels. Heavy box-section frame can be seen. Fenders are metal, body is plastic. Leslie in back of car.

Right hand side of "powerless" Leslie Special; exhaust stacks can be seen on hood sides, plus other brass baubles. Hannibal 8 lurks out in front.

This is the Troop Carrier Van made for the movie "Mega Force." It belonged to Fantasy Cars of El Cajon, California. They sold it to the Miami Beach Police Museum, where it is still exhibited. The museum also uses it for parades and special events.

The "Street Legal Tank Car" was built by Fantasy Cars to be used as a limousine. Before the company was able to rent it out, it was sold to the Miami Beach Police Museum to drive in parades and use in special promotional activities. The car is based on a 1964 Lincoln Continental four-door sedan. It features bullet-proofed parts, a roof-mounted cannon, and rocket launchers on the front fenders.

George Barris used the "T-Buggy" in a Sea World television special and it later appeared in several movies, including one starring Walter Brennan. It had a one-piece fiberglass body on a Volkswagen chassis with squared-off 1915 Model T-style fenders. The car is yellow with black and orange striping. George Barris offered it as a full-sized kit car and AMT was selected to manufacture a scale model kit based on it.

"This car needs some research," says Bob Butts of Fantasy Cars. "My information sources are good and I believe them to be true." According to Butts, the body was designed and carved by Pete Brock, who worked for Carroll Shelby. It was a proposal on a replacement for the GT-40 and two bodies were made. Both are now owned by Fantasy Cars. One body was assembled on a Volkswagen chassis for the movie "Ice Pirates." It was later repainted for its appearance in "Back to the Future II." Still later, it was seen in the television show "The Flash."

This is another of the famous George Barris television cars built for the "Munsters" show staring Fred Gwynne, Yvonne DeCarlo, Al Lewis, Butch Patrick and Pat Priest. Filmed in 1964 and 1965, this series was one of the highest-rated comedies of that era.

The Munster Koach was made by using three fiberglass replica Model T Ford bodies and stretching them out, tandem-style, for a 20-foot-long vehicle. A Ford Cobra V-8, built by Lou Senter of Ansen Automotive, powered the beast. It was painted Spider Webbed Black with brass trim and a Blood Red interior.

Robert Blake drove this customized 1967 Plymouth Barracuda in the film "Corky." It was also seen in commercials for batteries, tires and gasoline and played a big part in the "Knight Riders" television series in 1992. Fantasy Cars sold it to Byron Barrows of Milton, Pennsylvania who recently reported that he and his family were getting much enjoyment from owning the car.

This kit car was built by actor Steve McQueen for his movie "LeMans." It has a Volkswagen power plant with a turbocharger and nitrous fuel injector. Fantasy Cars repainted it and the car was then used in the movie "Herbie Goes to Monte Carlo." It can presently be seen at the Guiness Book of Records Museum in Gatlinburg, Tennessee.

The Monster Gator Car starred in the movie "Death Race 2000." It is owned by Fantasy Cars, which also has the "Bull Car" used in the same film. Both cars also were seen in the movie "Earth Girls are Easy" and in several music videos and television commercials.

This is one of two "Spinner" cars Fantasy Cars made for the motion picture "Blade Runner." One of them has been sold to the Miami Beach Police Museum. The other went to a museum in Japan. This car was painted in a very weird color scheme to make it look different for the film "Back to the Future II."

This is the customized truck and trailer that Fantasy Cars, of El Cajon, California, uses to haul cars back and forth to Hollywood movie studios. It is actually an old water truck built in 1982. It has a 366 cubic inch gasoline engine and a special automatic transmission with 16 forward speeds.

"The skull mounted on the wind-break of our trailer is from the movie 'Ice Pirates,'" says Bob Butts. "Our cost to customize the truck and trailer, back in 1987, was approximately $25,000. It is worth every penny spent, as the studios remember our name and the truck, which helps us get our share of the movie car business."

The Tedham Car seen here was built by a Phoenix, Arizona resident for his wife. After retiring in 1982, they relocated to Oregon and had no more use for the car. They sold it to Fantasy Cars, with the hopes they might see it in a movie. It appeared in the films "Condor" and "Back to the Future II." The Volkswagen-powered machine also appeared in the television show "The Flash." It has a tube chassis with dust panels installed on the bottom. "It is one of the better built cars in the Fantasy Car Collection," says owner Bob Butts.

The Sleeper Car was made for the movie "Sleeper" starring Woody Allen. It has been seen in many commercials and other motion pictures. One of its latest roles was in the film "Back to the Future II."

This "Chariot" built by Fantasy Cars is made up of four Honda Rebel motorcycles modified with molds taken from a carousel horse and placed over them. The throttle, gear shift, brakes and steering of the front two cycles are controlled from the chariot. The unit was finished by Fantasy Cars in mid-1992 and so far has been used in one Southern California city for a Fourth of July celebration, where it was a big hit.

The Robot Car was constructed by Fantasy Cars for the movie "Second Series of Remo Williams" in which it was used as a Russian robot. It is hydraulically-operated so that it moves jerkily, rather than in smooth movements. The arms move up and down, while the guns or hands on the arms move left and right on one side and up and down on the other. The head is a clear bubble which has a blood-colored substance running through clear veins. The head also moves up and down approximately two and one-half feet.

The O'Henry Car was named after a gentleman named Henry who started building it. Unfortunately, he passed away soon after completing the chassis. Fantasy Cars finished construction in late-1992. It has not been leased out yet. The movie-car company plans on mounting guns or missiles on the roof. The doors open via electronic actuators.

This 1956 Lincoln-Continental originally belonged to news commentator and actor Alex Drier of Chicago, Illinois. It was modified with a push-button double-bubble roof, vertical grille, four bucket seats, television, phone, stereo and fur carpets. It wound up at an auto museum owned by Art Grandlich in Apache Junction, Arizona. They sold it to Fantasy Cars. It appeared in the movie "Condor."

This is the Project 2000 Car. In the 1980s, investors put up $80,000 to design and build a prototype vehicle for possible marketing. They had several good ideas, such as unbolting the back half of the car and bolting on pickup or station wagon bodies included in the purchase price. Unfortunately, the $80,000 was used up before completion of the car. Fantasy Cars bought the car in unfinished condition and completed it to its current format. It was seen in "Back to the Future II," the "Flash" and several other media productions.

Designed by George Barris, the Turbo-Sonic was envisioned as a three-wheeled race car of the future. It was used in the movie "Garage A Go-Go" starring Tom Jones and Walter Brennan and later appeared in "Back to the Future II." The power plant, a 50-pound fuel-burning 1,000-horsepower turbine, was stolen while the car was in storage. It's now in the Fantasy Car Collection.

This futuristic bus took the "Jack Conrad Band" on tour in a motion picture. It was constructed on a 1939 White chassis. Notice the aeronautical design, heavy streamlining, whitewall tires and skirted rear fenders. Those traffic cops must have had a hard time catching up with this rocket ship.

Auto historian Don Wood sent in this photo with a challenge. "Your readers will have to help identify this make of car," he wrote. "It appeared in B.F. Goodrich television commercials." We guess that it's a "Thin Air Mobile" or an "Invisible V-8." What do you think?

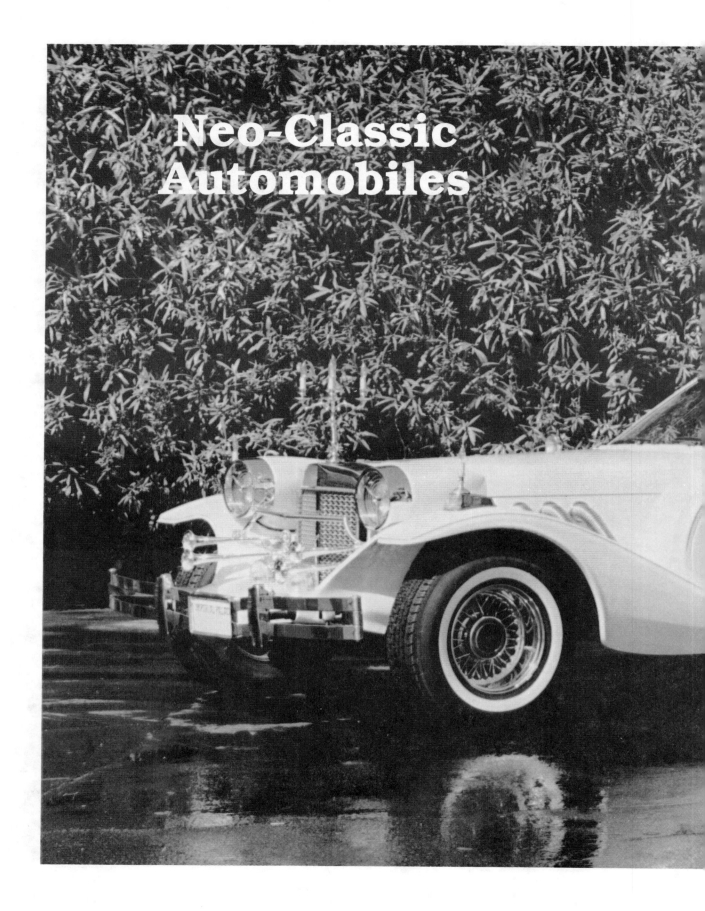

Neo-Classic
Automobiles

This 1981 Zimmer Golden Spirit was modified for entertainer Liberace. Among its weird features is a full-sized candelabrum fitted as a radiator ornament. There are two more candelabra on the vehicle, one on each side. Inside are several glow-in-the-dark candelabra and flower vases. "All in all it's so extravagant even Elton John might consider it ostentatious," said OLD CARS' British correspondent Dave Selby when the car appeared at a classic car show in England. It is part of the Imperial Palace Auto Collection. Apparently, even this car doesn't seem too gaudy in Las Vegas.

William M. Saeman of Sun City, Arizona, believes that his 1986 Continental Royale is one of only six of these models built by Handcrafted Motorcars, Incorporated of Florida. He describes it as a "neo-exotic sports car" and "a fine example of American ingenuity in the smaller automobile shops." The car is styled like a Golden Spirit, but built to a larger scale. It has a 156-inch wheelbase and is eight inches wider than a 1986 Lincoln.

Powering the Continental Royale is a reworked 460 cubic-inch Lincoln engine. It has a beige leather interior and Tru-Spoke wire wheels. Each of these cars has slight differences. This makes each of them unique and distinctive. Bill Saeman's car has 5,900 miles. He adds the amazing fact that none of the six cars built has ever been on the West Coast. No wonder they didn't sell!

The Phariance was a modern rendition of a famous old classic car made by Hispano-Suiza, which is known as the Tulipwood Roadster. The manufacturer of this neo-classic was Camelot Classics Corporation. This firm was founded, in Ventura, California, by Fritz R. Huntsinger and Ray Kinney. They described it as "automotive sculpture" and said that it was constructed of the finest hickory, Honduran mahogany and brass over a two-year period.

Bob Butts, of Fantasy Cars, drove this neo-classic across the United States for several years. He used it to make trips to places as far away as Florida to purchase vehicles for his El Cajon, California-based movie car company. It was even used as a tow vehicle. The customized 1974 Ford LTD would attract car enthusiasts wherever he went and helped him get leads on special cars to buy.

The Spartan Two-Plus-Two Roadster was a neo-classic built by International Automobiles of West New York, New Jersey. It represents the company's vision of classic styling motifs on a modern chassis.

In the early 1980s, Dunham Coach Corporation marketed a car that looked like a Rolls-Royce. It wasn't. The running gear came from General Motors and the engine was a 350 cubic inch four-barrel V-8. The Dunham Coach had a 98-inch wheelbase and overall length of 185.3 inches. It was 69 inches wide and 48 inches high.

Panther Westwinds was an English firm that manufactured two high-quality neo-classics on Jaguar running gear around 1979. The Panther DeVille was a four-door sedan with a long 142-inch wheelbase. Its V-12 engine generated 244 horsepower. Its top speed was claimed to be 128 miles per hour. The car was a loose copy of the Bugatti Royale. It sold for about $92,000.

This is not a neo-classic. It's a capital "C" Classic ... the 1931-1932 Bugatti Royale 41111 Henri Binder Coupe de Ville. Comparing this photograph to the picture above, you can see the design relationship of the two vehicles. Only six Bugatti Royales were made. They were among the largest cars ever built. Sales to royalty were anticipated, although never realized. This car was in Bill Harrah's museum and is now part of the General William Lyons Collection in Newport Beach, California.

"Here are photographs for your new publication 'Weird Cars,'" wrote Elustra S.J. Johnson of Crystal Lake, Illinois. "This is my 1969 Palmeri Touring Car, which has been called weird because of its slanted top. My fellow auto enthusiasts call her weird, awesome, macabre, cool and beautiful." She included a drawing indicating that the Palmeri is 170 inches long, 79 inches wide and 74 inches high.

The 1969 Palmeri was designed and built by Antonio (Tony) Palmeri in a two car garage behind his home in East Detroit, Michigan. He was a tool and die maker who built several individualized vehicles which resembled the fiberglass kit cars of that era. The car is made of steel taken from old Cadillacs and has a 1969 Chevrolet Biscayne chassis and V-8 engine. It cost $10,000 to build.

Owner Modified Cars

Owner modified automobiles can be inspired by art statement cars, custom cars, and dozens of other types of cars. They generally reflect "back yard" attempts to achieve the same type of goals that professional shops realize in personalizing a vehicle. The owner modifications can range from unusual paint jobs to strange "accessories" hung on their cars. Whatever the changes, the end results often turn out to be weird cars.

Professor Philip C. Campbell spotted this old 1930s Citröen in Mallorca, Spain, where it was being used to advertise the Ca'l Dimoni Restaurante. The car caught the eye of many passing tourists and the big arrow that the owner attached to the roof pointed them in the right direction. The strange "PM" license plate is for Mallorca.

Leo Frank of Shawano, Wisconsin built this "woody," which caused quite a stir at the Iola Old Car Show a few years ago. The fenders, cowl and bumpers are made of old barn boards. He used a 1957 Plymouth frame, a 1957 Chrysler 392 cubic-inch hemi V-8 engine and a 1967 Dodge four-speed transmission. It is registered as a street-legal vehicle.

Bill Pettit, the curator of the city museum in New London, Wisconsin, sent this picture of his "father's Oldsmobile." Actually, the 1923 touring car was owned by his stepfather who decorated it with a large sign advertising a cross-country trip that the family took through 20 states, plus Mexico and British Columbia. Mementos and artifacts gathered along the way were hung on the car.

Here's the car that started "Kenny's Clunkers." OLD CARS research editor Ken Buttolph paid $15 for the 1952 Dodge sedan. When he spotted a Lakeland College sticker on the window, he decided to play a joke on his friend Terry Boyce, an automotive writer who had moved to Lakeland, Florida. Obtaining a beat up row boat, old fishing rods, a fish-shaped sign and other items, Buttolph decorated the Dodge and displayed it at the Iola Car Show, which Boyce was attending with his wife Sally. Buick dealer Wally Rank saw the laughs it got from the crowd and invited Kenny to bring his clunker to his Milwaukee car show.

Close-up look at front end.

This weird-looking stretched wheelbase Lincoln was spotted in Los Angeles by photographer Robert Frumpkin. The car has just about every type of accessory that has ever been offered to home customizers, including a Rolls-Royce type grille, external exhaust pipes, vinyl roof and Lucas-style headlamps.

Rear view of the long Lincoln shows a few additional modifications that the owner has made to the car, including chrome deck lid straps, running boards, fender flares and a continental spare tire. The car also has a television inside, judging by the antenna in the center of the deck lid. This is a one-of-a-kind machine and it's no wonder.

Whitney Miller of College Place, Washington was 12 when he started collecting coins. In 1957, he decided to cover a car with coins, but had only enough to make an outline on one door. By 1964, his car had been decorated with 12,000 coins from every country in the world, plus $3,000 worth of U.S. coins. They were cemented to the inside and the outside of the vehicle, a 1927 Dodge. The coins added 400 pounds to the weight of the Dodge sedan.

Miller toured the country in 1964, covering 27 states and 8,726 miles visiting the Lions International convention in Toronto, Canada and the headquarters of the fraternal organization in Chicago, Illinois. The tour was sponsored by the Lions Club of College Place, Washington. He traveled from Chicago to the New York World's Fair, then on to the 73rd annual American Numismatic Association convention in Cleveland, Ohio. In Niagara Falls, Canada, Miller was offered a deal by a museum owner who was willing to trade the Al Capone Cadillac (now in the Imperial Palace Auto Collection) for the coin-covered Dodge.

Appearing at the first Carlisle Imports Show was this Peugeot station wagon with a zebra stripe paint job that looked like it had been modified for use on an African safari. The weird paint job was accented by the cow skull hood ornament.

This owner-modified Oldsmobile showed up at the Antique Automobile Club of American Eastern National Meet at Hershey, Pennsylvania during October 1988. Someone had done a nice job modifying the 1955 Oldsmobile 98 two-door hardtop into an El Camino style pickup.

Here's a weird-looking owner-modified Mustang Mach 1 Sportsroof that you could have owned for a mere $2,500 (or best offer). It was for sale at the fall meet in Jefferson, Wisconsin in September 1990. As you can see, it has the special large diameter exhaust system!

Bill Glass of the House of Hubcaps in Seattle, Washington sent this photo of the 1959 Dodge he uses to advertise his business. Several years ago, Bill Glass put together a hubcap identification guide that would be very handy to have if you were faced with the job of identifying all the hubcaps and wheelcovers on this car.

Here's another zebra-striped car sent in by Manson Marks of Holiday, Florida. This one is a 1966 Ford four-door done up as a Surfmobile. Check out the plastic swan hood ornament. "Lifeguard on duty" says a sign on the rear fender, which is handy to know since a Ford ragtop lover might try to drown himself after seeing these owner modifications.

This is the opposite side of the Surfmobile, which is a real piece of art. It's decorated with a weird paint job and a number of stickers offering some thoughts-for-the-day to people who drive by. The slogans range from "WhY bE nOrMaL?" to "So it smokes ... so does your mother!" Note the arrow sticking out of the target painted on the rear deck lid.

Barnes Thunderbird Shop of Houston, Texas saved this "near-dead" 1957 two-seater from the scrap pile to celebrate the nation's bicentennial celebration on July 4, 1976. It has been used in a number of parades since then. Each time the car is specially repainted for the occasion: St. Patrick's Day, Thanksgiving, Christmas, Frontier Days and so on. It has had 33 paint jobs in the past 17 years. What a "funeral" for a '57 T-bird!

Steven D. Zwack of St. Louis Park, Minnesota built this weird and wonderful Oldsmobile ragtop. It started life as a 1967 Oldsmobile 98 convertible. A 1959 Oldsmobile 98 rear clip was attached to the 1967 front end. The body was extended three feet for a total length of 20 feet. To top off the work, a 1955 Oldsmobile hood ornament was used.

Product Mobiles

The Wienermobile (above) is the most famous of all productmobiles, with a long history dating back to 1936. Other examples of "rolling billboards" seen here include the Meineke Mufflermobile, a Moxie Horsemobile, the 1923 Model T Mobile Home Car and an Outspan Orange Car from England's National Motor Museum.

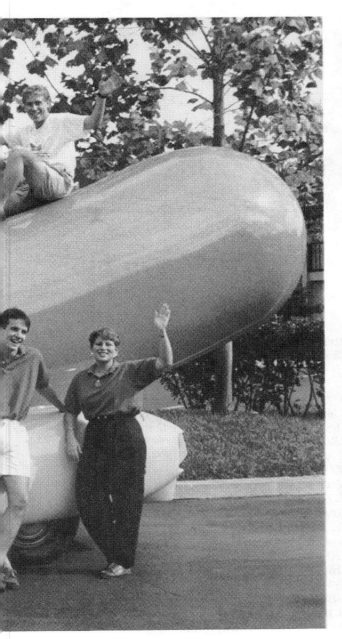

Top 25 Productmobiles

The Weinermobile is one of the top 25 Productmobiles.

1. Weinermobile
   Various platforms
2. Moxie-mobile
   1927 LaSalle
3. Outspan Orange Car
   1972 Mini
4. Meineke Muffler Car
   Mini-pickup truck
5. Bevo Boat (Anheuser-Busch
   Brewery Company)
   Pierce-Arrow
6. Worthington Bottle Car
   1924 Daimler
7. Zippo Windproof Lighter Car
   1948 Chrysler
8. Pep-O-Mint Life Savers Mobile
   1934 Dodge Truck
9. Quaker Oats Car
   1926 Auburn
10. Thermos Bottle Mobile
    1910 Truck
11. Stroh's Beer Can Car
    1980s hot rod
12. Creamobiles (sold to dairies)
    1935 Dodge Trucks

13. Mrs. Stover's California
    Bungalow Candies
    1929 Fargo Truck
14. Nu-Grape Soda Car
    1925 Chevrolet (Mercury body)
15. Planters Salted Peanuts Car
    1927 Dodge (Millspaugh & Irish body)
16. Blony Chewing Gum Mobile
    1934 Dodge Truck
17. Electrolux Vacuum Cleaner Car
    1922 Morris Cowley
18. Florida Orange Juice Mobile
    1930 Ford Model A truck
19. Warner Auto-Meter Car
    1907 Stoddard-Dayton
20. Airwalk Shoe Mobile
    Hot rod
21. Bowling Pin Car
    1920s Studebaker
22. Chicken Dinner Candy Bar Mobile
    1954 Ford F-100 Pickup
23. V-8 Vegetable Juice Car
    Hot rod
24. Quaker Photo Camera Mobile
    1925 Chevrolet truck
25. House Car
    Model T Ford Roadster

Shown here are various types of bodies produced by the Vehicle Department.

A Bus Body

"The Bevo Boat" Which Was to Tour the Country on Recruiting Drives in War Time

A Bigger and Better "Bevo Boat."

Horse Van

A Superior Refrigerated Truck Body

Anheuser-Busch, the St. Louis brewer, maintained its own vehicle-building department for many years. It produced such things as a bus body, a fleet of Bevo Boat cars, a barn-shaped horse van and refrigerated truck bodies. The department also built Henry Ford's well-known Lamsteed Camping Car on a Model T Ford chassis. This camper was part of Bill Harrah's famous automobile collection for many years.

As you can see on the side of the bow, this Bevo Boat was actually christened "The Budweiser." The car was wearing 1931 Missouri license plates when this photo was taken at the Indianapolis Motor Speedway. The man sitting in the rear seat is Captain Eddie Rickenbacker, the World War I flying ace who was also the owner of the speedway.

Race drivers Barney Oldfield (front) and Earl Copper and Tommy Milton (rear) were passengers in the Budweiser boat car when it visited the 500-mile race in May 1931. This Bevo Boat car rides a Pierce-Arrow chassis. Among the special nautical features are four small cannons, life preservers, a rudder, an anchor and front and rear flagstaffs.

The passenger may be Tony Cabooch, judging by the name on the pennant. (Indianapolis Motor Speedway Corporation photo.)

Land Cruiser and Boat Cars by Bud

By Paul Hatmon

There's an old Quaker saying which states: "I've begun to believe everyone in the world is peculiar but me and thee, and just lately I've began to wonder about thee." This is especially true for the people who build custom auto bodies. I'm not talking of the ordinary type of car bodies, but those shaped like candy rolls, ice cream bars, houses, light bulbs, huge bees, choo-choo trains and the topper, which I saw last fall in a parade, a mattress on wheels.

One of the most peculiar advertising gimmicks related to wheeled vehicles appeared in the post World War I era. This was the Bevo Boat, a ship-shaped automobile made by the Anheuser-Busch Company of St. Louis, Missouri.

With the arrival of Prohibition in 1920, the famous brewer decided to market a new, non-alcoholic concoction of barley malt, rice, hops, yeast and water. It was called Bevo, from the Bohemian word "privo" for beer. To advertise this product, the company commissioned a truck body firm to build a luxury type, inboard cruiser boat body. It was then mounted on a car chassis.

The Bevo Boat was equipped with the finest appointments and detailed with leather upholstery, thick carpets and fine woods. It seemed to be a luxury wagon in every manner of speaking. Eventually, it was even radio-equipped.

This Bevo Boat served many purposes. Anheuser-Busch used the odd-shaped vehicle to exploit its wares to receptive and thirsty Midwesterners. It was also employed to promote sales of government bonds. With so much to do, the vehicle became just the first in a fleet of boat-shaped productmobiles built by the beer company.

207

All of the boat cars built by Anheuser-Busch Company drew large crowds whenever they were seen in promotional appearances. Some of the Bevo Boats were employed to help sell United States War Bonds. (IMSC photo).

History is somewhat hazy on exactly how many more Bevo Boats were built. Following the Armistice, at least two more were constructed. The newest of these was completed in the mid-1920s. When Prohibition was repealed in 1933, the productmobiles were rechristened "Budweiser Cars."

One old photo, snapped prior to renaming the cars, shows a dapper young gentleman posing stiffly for a photographer behind the wheel of one of these fine, highly-polished machines. The flag of the beer company flies at the masthead. The American flag appears at the stern. The boat-car is fully equipped with a propeller in back, twin anchors in front, lifesavers on either side and cannons all over. There are small cannons mounted on both rear fenders, one on the hood and another on the rear deck. (The reason for the cannons has not come to light, unless it was to shoot down the competing brewers.)

In the mid-1930s, one of these land cruisers appeared at Indianapolis Motor Speedway. It was photographed extensively by track photographers. (Copies of the photographs are still available, at reasonable cost, from the IMSC photo department at 317-241-2501). One picture showed race car drivers Earl Cooper, Tommy Milton and Barney Oldfield as passengers in the boat-car. Another showed it parked near a Rickenbacker automobile, named after speedway owner Eddie Rickenbacker.

At least one Bevo Boat survived. In the late 1960s, a classic car enthusiast from Kansas City, Kansas was on a trip to Arkansas. James Pearson, a collector widely known for his Cadillac V-8s, V-12s and V-16s, was in pursuit of other rare birds when he encountered the Bevo Boat. It was not in quite the same condition in which it had been launched. In fact, it was pretty worn out.

Initially, Pearson was most interested in what the boat-car was sitting on. Under it was a 1932 Cadillac Model 370B V-12 long-wheelbase (140 inches) chassis. Pearson purchased the venerable old relic. Since it couldn't maneuver under its own steam, he towed it home to Kansas City.

Pearson researched the car through the Anheuser-Busch archives and other sources. According to information available from the company at that time, it had been built on a Pierce-Arrow chassis. Other facts that came to light revealed that its original chassis was within an inch or two of being the same length as that of the big Cadillac. Where the Cadillac running gear came from, or where and when the swap was made, no one seemed to know.

The body fit the Cadillac chassis perfectly. It looked as if it could have been built for it. The Cadillac V-12 fit under the body and all the instruments were of the type that Cadillac used. However, below the hood where the radiator frame support was located, was a standard piece of Pierce-Arrow equipment that proved the car had originated in Buffalo, New York (home of the Pierce-Arrow Motor Car Company).

Pearson planned a professional restoration of the boat-car and registered it with the Classic Car Club of America in the 1970s. In fact, he registered it as both a car and a boat at that time.

According to the Anheuser-Busch Company's archives today, a Bevo Boat was last known to be in Florida, which seems like a fitting location for such a vehicle. Apparently, this is the same car that Pearson discovered some 20 years ago.

What about the other Bevo Boats? No one seems to know much about their fate or whereabouts. Possibly they were gone long ago. Many unusual antique and classic cars were lost to scrap drives before or during World War II. On the other hand, one of the vehicles might be hiding in some rickety old barn ... or some rickety old boat house.

The Bevo Boats featured high-quality construction and the finest fittings and accessories. The Woodlites used on the front fenders went well with the nautical hardware such as anchors, cannons and life preserves. The driver was decked out like a real yachtsman with sea captain's hat and uniform. (IMSC photo).

Here's a real "T-house." This car, on display at the Belltown antique auto meet in East Hampton, Connecticut, is owned by a New England real estate dealer. The slogan "ready to move in" appears on the car today, according to photographer David S. Ebersole.

Here is the opposite side of the same Model T Ford reproduced from a newspaper clipping that shows an old postcard. W.H. Sawyer Lumber Company of Worcester County, Massachusetts used the fancy "mobile home" to promote its 52nd year in business during 1923.

England's first bottle car appeared in 1906. The well-known Worthington Bottle Car is constructed on a 1924 Daimler Model TL30 chassis. Many of these were made, but only four or five are thought to survive. This one is an attraction at the National Motor Museum in Beaulieu Hants, England owned by Lord Montagu.

The Worthington Bottle Car's bottle sections are brown. The body is orange, the fenders are black, the label is red and white. A bottle cap is visible above the radiator. The truck sold for 950 pounds. This model was built from 1919 to 1925. It has a 4962 cc six and top speed of 45 miles per hour.

This is a real camera body. Quaker Photo Services, a commercial photography business in Philadelphia, Pennsylvania used this 1925 Chevrolet productmobile to advertise. In Wisconsin, the MILWAUKEE JOURNAL also had a Model T with a body shaped like a Graflex camera. It had a complete mobile darkroom inside.

In 1926, this specialty car was built by the Auburn Automobile Company of Auburn, Indiana. It was used to promote sales of Quaker Oat products, which were advertised as "foods shot from guns." A cannon on the rear of the Auburn touring car shot the puffed wheat or puffed rice into the glass "gazebo."

Moxie started out as a patent medicine and became a carbonated soft drink in the 1920s. The Moxiemobile evolved from a horse-drawn bottle-shaped wagon that the company used for promotions. Though the prototype was made on a chassis from a small car called the Dort, the Moxie Beverage Company preferred using fancier cars such as this 1928 LaSalle for the fleet of productmobiles it built. The car is driven from the horse's back and is tricky to operate.

Moxiemobiles, like this Rolls-Royce, were driven by men wearing an English riding habit, boots, jockey cap and puttees. Special controls allowed steering, braking, gear shifting and acceleration to be handled from up in the saddle. The horses were fashioned of molded aluminum and painted white. They have real saddles and bridles. The Moxiemobiles were said to have attracted large crowds wherever they were taken to promote the tangy-tasting drink.

A true souvenir of Florida's "tin can tourist" era is this 1930 Ford Model A orange juice vending truck. It reflects the population boom in the Sunshine State during the Great Depression era. The truck was owned by Sam LaRoue, of Miami, when this photo was taken at its first car show appearance. The body is shaped like an old orange juice can.

Jeepneys are the colorful vehicles popular in the Phillipines. They combine aspects of Jeeps, custom cars, hot rods and sports-utility vehicles. This example was used as a promotional vehicle by the Tombstone Pizza Company.

Huston Ray, known as the "Music Healer" had a miniature piano specially-mounted on the rear bumper of his 1928 Auburn Model 8-115 boattail speedster. Mr. Ray was a novelty pianist in vaudeville productions. His assistant must be the famous "ragtime gal" we heard so much about years ago.

The product that the "Christopher Special" hoped to sell was the mayor of San Francisco. "Re-elect Mayor Christopher: A Good Mayor: He Gets Things Done" reads the sign on top of the locomotive-shaped car. The photo was taken in the summer of 1959. Makes you wonder if the voters felt that they had been "railroaded" after their ballots were cast and counted!

This scale model built by Brooks Stevens & Associates shows what the 1988 Wienermobile looked like as it developed into its final shape and format. The Milwaukee industrial design firm helped build six of the hot dog-shaped vehicles on 1988 Chevrolet van chassis to tour the United States. Thirty years earlier, Brooks Stevens had created the only Wienermobile based on a Jeep.

The 1988 Wienermobiles were 23 feet long, eight feet wide and 10 feet high. The fiberglass body featured a sun roof and gull-wing door. A Chevrolet V-6 powered the 5,800-pound vehicles. Inside they had refrigerators, microwaves, cellular phones and hot dog steamers which emitted the aroma of freshly cooked wieners to entice passers-by. Employees who take these famous productmobiles around the country say it's wise to "watch your buns" when you are behind the wheel. Six different generations of Wienermobiles have been seen over the years since 1936. The oldest known to exist today is a 1952 model that entered the Henry Ford Museum collection during 1992.

Six of the sixth-generation Wienermobiles built in 1988 are seen here. They extended a tradition that began in 1936. Brooks Stevens' Wienermobile of 1958 was the first to put the hot dog on a bun. Prior to that the wiener was towed behind on a trailer. These Wienermobiles made a nationwide hometown tour.

The 1988 models were driven on their cross-country tours by 12 recent college graduates called "hot doggers." They were said to "relish" their job as Oscar Mayer's goodwill ambassadors. They nicknamed the vehicles "Wiener-bagos." Four additional units were constructed for shipment to Spain and Japan.

Hot-Doggin' Through History

The oldest known survivor of early Wienermobile history is this unit that recently entered the Henry Ford Museum Collection.

First it was Little Oscar. Today, it's a customized van filled with recent college grads hot-doggin' their way through the big cities and small towns of America.

Twelve young people are selected each year to pilot six giant wienie wagons across the country. Serving as spokes people for Oscar Mayer Foods Corporation, the "Hot-doggers" (as they are known) go through extensive training before accepting the keys to one of the nation's best known corporate symbols ... the Oscar Mayer Wienermobile.

Rich in history and steeped in tradition, the Wienermobile has become a favorite with kids of all ages.

1936: It all began when a 13-foot metal hot dog was created by the General Body Company of Chicago, Illinois to transport the world's smallest chef. This original version featured open cockpits in the center and rear. Later, a glass enclosure was added for the driver's protection.

1950-1953: After the war, the program was reactivated and expanded to include each of the then operating Oscar Mayer plants. Five Wienermobiles were designed and built by Gerstenlager of Wooster, Ohio. Set on a Dodge chassis, these units were the first to have buns! They toured the country for many years and one of the fleet served as the prototype for the latest-generation Wienermobiles of 1988.

1958: A futuristic, bubble-nosed Wienermobile, designed by Brooks Stevens of Excaliber fame, was built by the Gisholt Company of Madison, Wisconsin. Incorporating some of the first fiberglass applications in the country, this unit was set on a Willys Jeep chassis. Unfortunately, it developed mechanical problems and was totally redesigned and rebuilt before retiring in the early 1960s.

1969: Two Wienermobiles were built by the Oscar Mayer mechanics in the garage at the company's headquarters in Madison, Wisconsin. Using a variety of automotive parts from numerous suppliers, these vehicles served the program well for many years. One unit now brings smiles to the people of Puerto Rico; the other is used occasionally for trade shows and special events in the United States.

1976: A Styrofoam and fiberglass unit, manufactured by Plastic Products of Milwaukee, Wisconsin, used the same mold as previous units. This time the unique hot dog-shaped car was mounted on a 1973 Chevy motorhome chassis. This Wienermobile resides in Spain, along with two of the 1988 models.

1988: Wienie wagons were brought back by popular demand. Six Wienermobiles were built on 1988 Chevy Van chassis with V-6 engines. They were designed to tour the country in style. Each 23-foot hot dog features a microwave oven, refrigerator, cellular phone and stereo system. They even have steam vents to emit the aroma of freshly grilled hot dogs. Nicknamed Yummy, Big Bun, Our Dog, Hot Dog, Weenr and Oscar, they create quite a stir when they pull into gas stations and supermarkets. Four additional Wienermobiles were built and shipped to Oscar Mayer affiliates in Spain and Japan.

Future: Harry Bradley, a renowned California auto designer, has created a Wienermobile concept vehicle for the year 2000. The longer, wider body still looks like a hot dog, although it has a sleeker, more contemporary appeal.

A dozen recent college graduates called Hot-doggers took the 1988 Wienermobiles on a summer whistle stop tour across the United States.

Photo of Wienermobile taken in Spain.   *Wienermobile at Madison "World of Wheels" show.*

219

"Major Video: The Super Video Store," is the wording painted on the side of this land-bound spaceship used to promote video casette rentals. It appears to be a three-wheeled vehicle. It looks somewhat like a jet aircraft engine pod with wheels, but photographer Jim Benjaminson had no details about it.

This photo was taken in The Netherlands." The barrel of Heineken on wheels looks like a "Dutch treat." We don't know if there is beer inside, but it's very unlikely. The vehicle is driveable. It has lights and a rear view mirror. There's also a bulb horn on top. The wheels look like beer bottle caps.

England's Outspan Organization built six advertising vehicles shaped like oranges between 1972 and 1974. The Outspan Orange Cars were based on Austin Minis. They used the same capable 998 cc four-cylinder engine, but recommended top speed was 30 miles per hour. Above that they tended to roll over.

Outspan Orange Cars appeared in promotions in England, France and Germany. One is still actively at work in South Africa. This example is at England's National Motor Museum Trust in Beaulieu Hants. The cars were made by Brian Waite Enterprises Ltd. They would go great with a Model A orange juice truck.

The Mufflermobile was built by Joe, Scott and Steve Minghenelli who operate Meineke Muffler shops in Berlin and Marlton, New Jersey. Joe and his sons started making muffler men and muffler dogs to display in their shops. Then they moved up to the big league. This car is 16 feet long and weighs a ton.

Based on a mini-pickup truck, the Mufflermobile project started with removal of all body panels, doors, fenders and the cargo bed. Then exhaust pipe was bent, cut and welded to the existing truck platform. This created a framework to hold 16-gauge steel panels, which were used to build the outer body.

The Stroh's Beer Can Car was on a widely distributed poster that depicted a shaggy dog driving it. This photo was taken at a car show in Fargo, North Dakota in May 1986. With its handsome roadster styling, it looks quite a bit like the V-8 Roadster that George Barris built to promote V-8 Vegetable juice.

Seen at a car show is the neat-looking Airwalk Shoe Car. It appears to be built on a dune buggy chassis with a Volkswagen engine in the rear. The headlamps and front turning lamps indicate it is street-driveable. There's a long history of shoe-shaped productmobiles dating back to a least the 1920s.

Quads

The first four-wheel-drive vehicles, sometimes called "quads," were built by the Four Wheel Drive Auto Company of Clintonville, Wisconsin. During World War I, the quads built by this firm and by Nash Motor Car Company served admirably as fighting vehicles.

Over the years, many weird quads have been constructed for work and play. Seen above is an artist's concept of the "Vehicle of the Decade" that appeared in a GMC Truck press kit. Naturally, this "truck for all seasons--for all reasons" is equipped with four-wheel drive. It is part standard pickup, part quad, part van, part suburban and part minivan.

Although we're unlikely to see such a rig actually built, this chapter shows that some weird quad-drive cars and trucks have been constructed.

"Thundernash" is the nickname for this Nash Airflyte four-wheel-drive. The famous Nash Quad was an early four-wheel-drive vehicle and this interesting four-door sedan could certainly be described as a Nash Quad. The custom front bumper treatment is particularly interesting.

With the ever increasing value of vintage Corvettes, the days of home-building four-wheel-drive versions may be over. This 1963 or 1964 convertible was photographed at a Corvette show in Jenkintown, Pennsylvania in 1978, when Corvette prices were a bit lower.

Larry Schwacofer and Sid Spaulding were the pilots of this four-wheel-drive off-road race car based on a 1955 Chevrolet two-door sedan. Here they are seen competing in the "Frontier 500," a 1983 event that ran through the desert between Las Vegas and Reno, Nevada.

If a "classic" 1955 Chevrolet can be turned into a four-wheel-drive race car, why not build a 1957 Nomad wagon that can go anywhere at anytime of the year? As you can see, somebody did just that. Then they decided to sell the car in an auction. The license plates on the front identify it as a "Sno-Mad."

The amazing "Grave Digger" is a four-wheel-drive exhibition vehicle that weighs more than six tons and rides on five-and-a-half-foot tires. This monster truck can soar 25 feet into the air before alighting on a row of jalopy cars. Dave Anderson of Chesapeake, Virginia spent $126,000 building it.

Okay ... so it's not really a quad. The "Six-Foot 6 X 6 X 6 Monster Truck" is still pretty weird. It measures 12 feet six inches high and wide and 22 feet six inches long. Goodyear supplied the 73 x 44 x 36 inch Terra tires. The truck is powered by a Chevy 454 cubic-inch V-8 with four-bolt mains linked to a Turbo-Hydramatic 400 transmission. The box and front end are hydraulically operated.

Only a handful of these Jeep Grand Wagoneer limousines were made in the late 1980s. This 1986 model showed up at an American Motors Owners Club convention in Minneapolis, Minnesota.

This four-wheel-drive race car has a weird history. Famed race car builder Harry Miller built it for the Four Wheel Drive Auto Company. Barney Oldfield test drove it. It raced at Indianapolis between 1932 and 1937. It was then retired to the FWD Museum in Clintonville, Wisconsin. In the early 1950s, Bill Milliken of Cornell Research Labs borrowed the car to compete in sports car races and the Pikes Peak Hillclimb. The 20-year-old car did great in both types of events. It still exists in a private race car collection.

John Calvert of San Gabriel, California, built the "Lunar Duner" in 90 days during 1967. He was 20 years old at the time. The 1957 Hillman featured a 430 cubic-inch Lincoln V-8, a four-speed transmission from a truck, homemade wheel rims and aircraft tires. The four-wheel drive vehicle was an outrageous sensation in the days before monster trucks.

Streamlined for speed was this Jeep with a "classy chassis." It was worked up by Technical Sargent Wayne K. Pike of Pittsburg, Kansas, while he was serving with the U.S. Army Air Force in the Netherlands, East Indies in August 1945. Pike used salvaged airplane parts to transform the military vehicle.

Racing Cars

What's so weird about racing cars? The above photo should answer that question. This drag-racing 1958 Plymouth Plaza station wagon was the subject of a feature article in a recent issue of MOPAR ACTION magazine. (Photo courtesy Cliff Gromer)

Ed "Big Daddy" Roth built the Yellow Fang Dragster in 1965. It featured a body by Tom Hanna. The power for the car was supplied by a hemi-head Chrysler Firepower V-8. It was claimed that the fuel-injected engine produced 900 horsepower. The car became part of Harrah's Automobile Collection when Harrah's became interested in unusual hot rods as a reflection of postwar American culture. The Yellow Fang Dragster, described as being in fair overall condition with fair paint and tires, was lot number 192 in Harrah's first liquidation sale held during 1984.

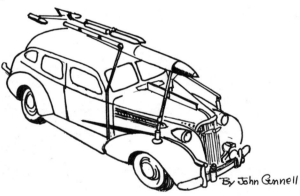

Jack Shelburne had the same idea as Fritz Opel: A rocket-powered car. He built it in Hannibal, MO in the '50s by strapping a rocket to the roof of a '37 Olds.

In 1928, Fritz Opel wanted to smash all world land speed records with his RAK 2 Opel rocket car. After igniting the 24 rockets in the rear of the sleek racer, his top speed was 233 kilometers per hour. The car is now a treasured part of the Opel Museum collection in Germany.

This unusual Indianapolis-style race car was specially built and owned by actor James Garner. It was designed to accommodate four people, rather than the usual single driver. Two passengers sit in bucket seats in the normal cockpit. Two additional bucket seats are housed inside the outrigger type body compartments just ahead of the rear wheels.

The rear view of the ex-James Garner four-place Indy car shows its unusual air-wing and open-top wheel-housings. The weird racing car allowed Garner to share his race-driving hobby with his friends. The car was recently restored by George W. Barber of Birmingham, Alabama.

Looking more like a land rocket than a car, the "Spirit of America" was the 1965 World Land Speed Record vehicle that Craig Breedlove constructed and drove. It used a jet-turbine engine that developed 6,800 pounds of thrust.

Sir Henry Seagrave went after the World Land Speed Record with his famous 1929 Golden Arrow. The car used a 12-cylinder Napier aircraft engine. It set the record with a fast run timed at 231 miles per hour at Daytona Beach, Florida. The persistent English driving ace wasn't satisfied. He brought the Golden Arrow back four times. Finally, in 1935, the car set a world's record of 276.820 miles per hour. The famous Chrysler Newport Phaeton (seen on the cover of WEIRD CARS in red) was originally supposed to be painted yellow and called the "Golden Arrow" after Seagrave's well-known machine.

"Count" Paul J. Kennedy's 1958 Plymouth Plaza wagon seems to have the special "Hearse Performance" trailering package. Some of the parts are said to have come from "Mr. Casket." According to Kennedy, the car was originally factory-modified especially for Richard Petty. It was later campaigned by the Golden Commandos drag racing team.

This drag racing "funny car" appears to be a "weirded-out" 1964 Mercury with a distorted grille and front bumper. Actually, the body is little more than a fiberglass shell on a rail-type frame and the front end components are a painting. That's right ... the headlamps, grille and bumpers are all an optical illusion created by a skilled graphic artist.

The Sunraycer, a solar-powered vehicle built by General Motors engineers, competed in the World Solar Challenge Race held in Australia during November 1987. It turned out to be the winner of the long-distance contest. Despite its insect-like looks, the vehicle proved to be the world's fastest sun-powered car. Later, the Sunraycer was put on display at the Smithsonian Institute's Museum of American History as a part of its permanent collection.

Before being enshrined in the Smithsonian, the Sunraycer went on an international tour where it was seen by engineers and scientists attending solar energy conferences. The car also visited science museums and elementary, high school and college campuses. Here we see a student entering the solar-powered race car's cockpit, which was accessible by removing the forward canopy. The car made its last trek in 1989 on a Michigan road course while competing in an event named GM Sunrayce USA.

The Auburn Cabin Speedster was created by Wade Morton, a test driver for the Auburn Automobile Company of Auburn, Indiana. His idea was to incorporate aerodynamic ideas he had learned from his aviation and high-speed driving experience into a racing car. It was based on a 1928 Auburn with a 115-inch wheelbase. The roof of the weird all-aluminum body was only 58 inches off the ground. The car's extreme lowness was aided by mounting the rear axle above the frame. The original car was destroyed in a blaze at the Los Angeles Automobile Show. Shown here is an exact reproduction of the original.

Famed race car builder Harry Miller designed an unorthodox race car called the Golden Submarine. It had an enclosed body that was said to be crash-proof. The press derogatively called it the "golden egg" and "golden lemon," but the weird became the wonderful when Barney Oldfield drove it. By the end of 1917, he held all dirt track records, but later it nearly became his "golden coffin" when he crashed in it.

(Above) The Mormon Meteor is an exotic Duesenberg that set many speed records. (Inset) The Mormon Meteor III coupe survives in Utah's state capitol.

Ab Jenkins and His Mormon Meteors

By Tom LaMarre

From 1932 to 1934, Ab Jenkins assaulted the 24-hour endurance record in a modified Pierce-Arrow V-12. His 112 miles per hour average speed in 1932 was an unofficial record. No official timer was present at the salt flats in Utah. However, one was on hand the next year, when Jenkins finished the 24-hour run with an average speed of 117.77 miles per hour with stops for fuel and tires.

In 1934, Jenkins pushed the Pierce-Arrow Special to a 127.229 miles per hour average speed. Under the heading "Utah Honors American Who Shatters World Records," the Firestone Tire & Rubber Company issued a press release saying, "Governor Henry H. Blood, of Utah, presented a cup to Ab Jenkins of Salt Lake City, famous American speed king, sportsman and automotive engineer for shattering 77 world, international and American Automobile Association (AAA) speed records on the Great Salt Desert of Utah. Hurtling through space for 24 hours, Jenkins traveled more than 3,000 miles at an average of 127.2 miles per hour, including stops. His tire, battery and spark plug equipment, made by Firestone, withstood the test, although the thermometer reached 120 degrees and holes in the salt bed had been filled with sharp-edged crushed rock."

The Pierce Special looked dated compared to the Duesenberg "Mormon Meteor" Jenkins drove in 1935. This custom-bodied record car was powered by a supercharged 380 horsepower SJ engine. It took three tries, but on June 6, 1935, Jenkins set a new 24-hour endurance record of 135.47 miles per hour. This time the "Iron Man" (as Jenkins was called) had the help of relief driver Tony Gulotta, the driver of Studebaker Indy race cars of that era.

Later, the fenders, body fin and other speed equipment were removed and the exotic Duesenberg was converted for street use. The Mormon Meteor now belongs to Knox Kershaw of Montgomery, Alabama. As for Ab Jenkins, by 1939 he drove the 850 horsepower Mormon Meteor III, breaking 45 speed records at Bonneville. Jenkins had more records than all other drivers combined. In 1939, he held 218 marks, ranging from the American 10-mile record to the world's 48-hour record.

This 1935 Mormon Meteor, also known as the Duesenberg Special Roadster, is a weird-looking racing version of the SJ model with a 380 horsepower supercharged engine. With Ab Jenkins behind the wheel, it completed a 24-hour endurance run at the Bonneville Salt Flats in Utah setting 218 speed records. Jenkins, a follower of the Mormon faith, also served as the Mayor of Salt Lake City. He drove the car without a relief driver. The 24-hour speed mark stood until just a few years ago, when a Corvette broke it. The car still survives in the collection of Knox Kershaw. There is also a Mormon Meteor coupe, which is kept in the capitol building in Salt Lake City.

Based on a Model A Duesenberg, this unusual vehicle was built to fuel the company's racing cars during non-stop endurance runs. The body has been removed at the rear to mount a fuel tank. The tender behind the safety rail would then fill the racing car while both vehicles were on the go.

Designed to be competitive in tractor pulling events, the Irish Challenger seems well-equipped for the job. It has five blown 604 cubic-inch Arias engines that each produce 1,800 horsepower. That puts a total of 9,000 horsepower on tap. Dave Walsh, the driver of the vehicle, earned "Puller of the Year" honors in 1989.

Art Afrons, the well-known drag racing star who campaigned the Green Monster jet dragsters in the 1950s, is now a force in the tractor pulling sport. He is the designer and driver of the twin turbine-powered modified tractor that's seen here pulling a 50,000 pound weight transfer sled towards the finish line at a national competition. As you might guess, the beer can-shaped body ties into the sponsor and this vehicle is called the "Busch Green Monster."

Ski-mobiles and Swim-mobiles

Going skiing with a car may sound like a weird thing to do. Taking your car for a dip in the water sounds even weirder. Nevertheless, auto designers have long been enchanted by the idea of a car that can slide across ice or swim through the water.

Virgil White's Snow Vehicles Were Fords

By A. Stanley Kramer

If you think the snowmobile is an outgrowth of the outboard engine, you're wrong, even though snowmobiles use high-revving two-cycle engines. According to the *ENCYCLOPEDIA BRITTANICA*, the first snowmobile was patented by Carl J. Elisson of Sayner, Wisconsin in 1927. This is an error. The snowmobile is several years older. Virgil D. White, of Ossipee, New Hampshire patented a workable snowmobile in 1917. He also manufactured and sold some 3,500 of them between 1923 and 1929.

Virgil White was a Ford dealer. His patents were for an attachment for an automobile which converted the car into a snow vehicle. Elisson, on the other hand, patented an entire vehicle. However, their concepts were essentially the same: A gasoline-powered vehicle, steered with runners and employing a tractor-like tread*.

The modern snowmobile (the name has been fought over by many and does not seem to be any company's property today) is a hybrid. It is part outboard motor, part sled and part motorcycle. It can go wherever there is snow hard enough to support it and needs no roads or special trails. There are many makes. They are fast (racers in special machines reach 90 miles per hour) noisy, unstable and undeniably thrilling as they shatter the stillness of field and forest, leaving behind the pall of fumes.

Snowmobiles have provided a whole new kind of winter outdoor family recreation including picnics, safaris and races. Their popularity really began in the mid-1960s and skyrocketed until the early 1970s. Then, the gasoline shortage slowed their growth.

They are easy to drive, steer with handlebars and have no gears to shift. A handle throttle (like that of a motorcycle) controls the speed of the cleated nylon or rubber belt that drives it. Coasting factor is about zero. Closing the throttle is like putting on brakes. As on a motorcycle, shifting one's weight helps control turns, skidding and jumps.

In the snow sports areas of North America, including New England, the Midwest, the Northwest and Canada, usage today extends far beyond being merely a fun vehicle. They are indispensable winter transport for forest rangers, policemen, mailmen and rescue operations and essential for ranchers, herders, trappers, hunters and fishermen.

In the far North, they have just about completely replaced the dog sled for carrying supplies, hunting, trapping and fishing. Eskimos use them for tracking caribou because they can track twice as far in a day as with a dog sled. One machine often pulls one or more heavily laden sleds.

All of this is a far cry from what Virgil White had in mind when he patented his car conversion and set up his New Hampshire factory to produce them. His basic idea was simplicity itself. He removed the front wheels from Model T roadsters and replaced them with skis. The wheels were then mounted at the rear, in front of the driving wheels to which they were attached by cleated, endless chain treads.

In White's day there was practically no dependable snow removal on New England's roads, and his machines made it possible to travel highways when the snow had stopped all other forms of transportation. His snowmobiles were strictly working transportation and not for sport. With a plow in front they often helped clear secondary roads. They traveled at a rattling but steady eighteen miles an hour, as sturdy and dependable as old Model T itself. There was nothing new for local residents to learn. Every one knew how to take care of his Ford. All the non-sportsman had to learn was how to wax skis.

Before White gave up his business (because large-scale snow removal road clearance was instituted in New England and he thought there would be no further market for his invention) he sold several of them to Arabs for use in the desert. How they ever managed to protect the skis' surfaces from the abrasion of the sand is an interesting question.

Somewhere in New England (we saw it many years ago) there is an interesting photograph of the funeral of Calvin Coolidge's father. The cortege consisted of a line of White's snowmobiles en route to the cemetery.

Some years after White closed his factory there was a move afoot to re-open it, but it was destroyed by fire and never rebuilt.

*Perhaps the grandfather of them both was Czar Nicholas pre-World War I Packard twin six with skis instead of front wheels.

This early snowmobile may be one of Virgil White's kits attached to an early Model T Ford equipped with winter enclosures. Whatever it is, the vehicle was used to deliver mail in Clayton, New York.

Here is another early snow tractor set-up used with a 1930 Ford Model A 1/2-ton pickup truck. It has an extra set of rear axles providing six rear wheels to carry the endless track. Up front, a sturdy pair of skis or runners is added. The truck has Minnesota license plates. Other Ford snow vehicles can be seen in the collection of the A-C-D Museum in Auburn, Indiana and at the Imperial Palace Auto Collection in Las Vegas, Nevada.

This huge Rolls-Royce touring car was built for the Russian dictator Lenin to drive in the winter at his rural enclave. It is of massive proportions with a wide endless track on the rear and giant-sized skis in front. Note that the skis are not attached to the axle, as with the Model A snow vehicle seen earlier. Instead, they are designed to accomodate the car's front tires in a bracket that clamps to the wheels and hubs. This car is one of four vehicles owned by Lenin that can be seen in Russian museums. There is also a very active antique car club in Russia.

Soviets Preserve Lenin's Auto

Three automobiles were associated with the name of Vladimir Lenin, the man who led the 1917 socilaist revolution in Russia and founded the Soviet state. They are kept in Soviet museums. Any car-loving visitor is welcome to take a look at them.

The weirdest among the three cars is a Rolls-Royce Silver Ghost seven-passenger model. It is kept at the Lenin Memorial House in Gorki, outside Moskow. That is where Lenin spent the closing days of his life.

Lenin used this car in 1919. It was specially modified for his winter rides. The rear wheels were replaced by rubber belt-tracks. This allowed the car to be driven nearly anywhere during the harsh Russian winters.

The Rolls-Royce "snowmobile" was designed by Adolphe Kegresse. He was a French inventor who worked in Russia. This made the huge car truly an international project, involving products and personalities from three nations.

A replica of the famous Citröen half-tracks was exhibited at European auto shows, such as the Veedol Starparade in Germany where this photo was taken.

Unusual Citröen

By John Gunnell

In 1931, a crew of daring adventurers set out on the Citröen automobile Company's Central Asia Expedition. Driving a fleet of 14 Citröen-built half-tracks, some 40 men took part in this remarkable effort to retrace explorer Marco Polo's famous "Silk Road" between the Mediterranean Ocean and the China Sea.

The expedition was split into two different crews. The first was called the Pamir Group. It traveled east from Beirut, over the Himalayas, towards a planned rendezvous in the Sin Kiang region of China. The second contingent was called the China Group. It traveled west from Peking, through the Gobi Desert, to reach the Sin Kiang area. After joining together, the adventurers were to return to Peking.

Georges-Marie Haardt was the man heading the Pamir Group. It had taken him two years, with help from Citröen, to make arrangements for the expedition. Neither the adventurer or the automaker, however, anticipated the various difficulties met during the trip.

The main barrier that both groups had to deal with was natural geographical obstacles. First, there was the sheer length of the route. Nearly 7,500 miles lay between the Mideast and China. For the Pamir Group, the 13,000-foot height of the Himalaya Mountains was another factor to be reckoned with. The China Group faced other problems, such as burning hot desert days and freezing cold desert nights.

There were additional difficulties of the human type. They included a revolution in Afghanistan, a war in China and political dissidence in the Sin Kiang region. Although countless time had been spent obtaining official authorizations and clearances, the soldiers and bureaucrats wielding power in the countryside caused a variety of delays and drawbacks.

In China, the warring factions of Chiang Kai Shek and the Kuomintang often cast aside the government promises of safe passage. Victor Point was head of the China Group. He noted that the early stages of the journey required "great patience." Upon entering Mongolia, a delegation of Chinese scientists joined the adventurers and often hindered their progress.

In Sin Kiang, the group ran into a problem with the ruler of the territory, President King. Citröen had promised him a gift of three half-tracks, but they had been taken by bandits. Consequently, the travelers were not allowed passports and were taken into "protective custody." They were prevented from wiring for help until they decided to celebrate a make-believe holiday. While his companions noisily honored the "Centenary of the Third Republic" the radio operator hid under one of the half-tracks and used Morse-code to contact a French sloop. French diplomats applied the necessary political clout to get Victor Point's party released.

The half-tracks used on the expedition carried 1,750 gallons of fuel, full rations and countless types of equipment. Each had enough supplies to last 1,250 miles. Being weighed down with all of this was enough to put the machines to the ultimate test. In addition, there was the constant threat of explosion, should a spark or lightning bolt hit the fuel containers.

Weather conditions and the general roughness of the terrain were additional challenges. The men faced sandstorms, snow, excessive heat and constant rain with electrical storms. Snow on the Bourzil Pass (elevation 13,750 feet) brought the danger of half-tracks sliding and skidding down the narrow mountain passages. At some points the paths measured just 50-1/2 inches. The vehicles were five inches wider than that. One half-track had the ledge below it give way but miraculously remained perched over a sheer drop of over 65 feet.

The vehicles moved along at speeds as low as three miles per hour and contended with steep slopes, natural obstacles, mechanical problems and crossing over 45 rickety wooden bridges. In some cases, block-and-tackle techniques were used to drag them. In other cases, the half-tracks were disassembled, carried by men, and reassembled on the opposite side of a mountain.

On the way back to Peking, after rendezvousing in Aksou in the seventh month, problems with Sin Kiang's President King surfaced again. He hadn't yet received his payment from Citröen and forced the expedition to halt at Ouroumtsi. On December 2, 1931, some eight months after the start of the journey, the gifts were received and the 40 adventurers were given passports and clearance to continue to Peking. This meant crossing the Gobi Desert again.

It was February 12, 1932 when the expedition entered the City of Peking. The great trek had been successfully completed, but the problems did not end. In Hong Kong, Georges-Marie Haardt was stricken with double pneumonia and died. Citröen telegraphed the rest of the party an inspirational message. "The man is dead, but his work lives forever," it said. "I weep for him with you."

Today, most of the brave adventurers are dead, but memories of their expedition still survive. Six of the Citröen half-tracks were taken to Alberta, Canada in 1933 to participate in an expedition from Edmonton, Alberta to Alaska, which was headed and financed by Charles Bedaux. The roughness of the Canadian terrain caused this effort to be abandoned and the half-tracks were left in British Columbia. One was later obtained by the Stanley G. Reynolds Museum in Wetaskiwin, Alberta and survives in the collection today. In addition, Citröen has constructed a replica of the Himalayan half-tracks.

Funny Car Facts

This is the 1926 Buick water taxi that Izzy Cholfin of Somerville, Massachusetts, operated on the Charles River. It could do 10 miles per hour in the water.

This automotive curiosity is powered by a three-cylinder gas engine. It was constructed in Jessup, Iowa by a Mr. T. Richmond in 1905. His design included a set of paddles to attach to the wheels when the vehicle was in the water. To make it into an ice boat, there were spikes to attach to the drive wheel. There was also a detachable runner for driving on ice.

The Delia Amphibian was created by Michael de Cosmo of San Francisco in 1916. It was also called the "Motor Duck." When the car was used in the water, the driver switched a lever that engaged a friction wheel. This mechanism operated a prop shaft. It had a rudder attached to the rear for steering in water. According to reports of the day, it could do about 10 miles per hour in the water.

George Monnot's Hydrocar "floated" on to the automobile scene in Canton, Ohio in 1917. It was designed to operate backwards in water. A Hercules four-cylinder engine supplied power to a propellor mounted up front, near the radiator grille. The boattail back end was perfect for cutting through the water of Meyers Lake, near Canton. It had a steering wheel at each end.

Here is another view of the Hydrocar. This was no "watered-down" machine, being of rather large size and ungainly proportions. Two prototypes were actually constructed. They could do about 25 miles per hour on land and nine miles per hour in the water. A company was formed to build production models, possibly for military use, but the U.S. Army wasn't interested.

This West Coast amphibious car was called the Hydromotor. It was designed by William Massei and William F. Purcell of Los Angeles, California. The Automobile Boat Manufacturing Company of Seattle, Washington agreed to build it. The car was tested at the Panama-Pacific Exposition in San Francisco in 1915. It had a 16-inch propeller and drove in the same direction on land or sea.

Paul Pankotan called the vehicle he patented an "Auto-Boat" and hoped to interest a company in manufacturing it. The engine used in the 1940 Pankotan produced 90 horsepower and was said to provide speeds up to 90 miles per hour on land. In the water, 35 miles per hour was claimed. By shifting a lever, the operator could raise the wheels above water level, allowing the car to float like a boat. Unfortunately, the inventor from Miami, Florida had little luck selling his idea.

Here's a bird that swims and is worth about $19,000 to a military vehicle collector. The GMC DUKW ... or "Duck" ... was a World War II amphibious six-wheel drive vehicle with a boat-type hull. It was built on a modified GMC channel-type truck frame and used a 270 cubic-inch GMC six-cylinder engine. A five-speed manual transmission was provided. A fleet of these vehicles have been used for the popular "Duck Boat" sight-seeing rides at the Wisconsin Dells amusement area, in Wisconsin, for many years.

Probably the best known of all "swim-mobiles" is the Amphicar. It first appeared during 1961 from a West German company. "Anyone who can drive a car can operate the Amphicar as a car or a boat," said the brochure. To use it as a boat, you simply drove into the water and switched on the twin screws that provided water propulsion. About 800 of the $3,995 vehicles were made and some 80 percent were sold in the United States.

Three-Wheel Cars

1897 Pennington three-wheeler.

1895 Reid Electric three-wheeler.

1991 Dorran three-wheeler.

1982 Ultra-Sport Tri-Magnum.

Entertainer Vic Hyde is a well-known collector of three-wheel cars. He uses this 1954 Tempo in parades. The German-made flatbed farm truck has a circus calliope mounted. His wife Sue drives, while he blasts out music at the Wisconsin State Fair.

251

Mrs. Everett S. Calhoun, wife of Davis' Seattle distributor, drives a Davis Motor Car in March 1949.

Remember the Davis?

By Richard Kelly

The three-wheeled Davis Car of 1947-1949 was one of dozens of new designs which burst from the drafting boards to fill the demands of a car-famished public just after World War II. Fledgling entrepreneurs offered new features strange to American car-buyers. There were cars with air-cooled engines, with front-wheel-drive, with rear-mounted engines, even with your choice of front- or rear-mounted engine on the same make and model. But, the Davis was a completely new idea and might have gone into successful production had not lack of financing and a confused management done it in.

Like many innovations, the Davis was born in Southern California. The story really begins with a one-off project designed and built just before the war by Frank Kurtis. Kurtis is a big name in American automobile racing. During the 1950s, the Indianapolis 500 was usually wall-to-wall Kurtis Kraft cars. In 1953 alone, the first 13 cars across the finish line, plus 12 more scattered among the starters, came from the small Kurtis plant in Glendale.

During the late 1940s, Kurtis had what amounted to an assembly line turning out midget race cars and built over 1,100 of them, usually powering them with Offy or Ford V-8 60 engines. And, of course, Kurtis is the creator of the roadster which later became the Muntz Jet and was the builder of the Kurtis Sports Car, the track-based design which terrorized the Jags and Allards in the halcyon days of semi-amateur sports car racing of the early 1950s.

In 1940, however, Kurtis was managing Joel Thorne's Burbank engineering shop. During slack periods he turned out several interesting projects. One was a replica Army jeep using a Model A Ford engine and running gear, a hand-built body and disc wheels. The car was in great demand for war movies by studios unable to get the real thing.

More important to the Davis saga, Kurtis worked up a modernistic little three-wheel roadster using the V-8 60 engine, transmission and rear end from a 1937 Ford. He added midget race car wheels and a Kurtis-designed-and-fabricated single front-

Gary Davis in the first prototype Davis three-wheeler near the Ambassador Hotel in November 1947.

wheel assembly, all wrapped in a sleek, streamlined body hand-formed by Kurtis. Thorne was delighted with the little car and drove it everywhere.

Enter Gary Davis, a one-time builder of custom-bodied cars for the movie set and promoter par excellence. Davis saw in the three-wheeler his chance to provide a unique answer to America's postwar transportation needs and in 1945 bought the little car. Thorne called it "The Californian," but the car's title listed it simply as a 1937 Ford. Davis used it as the basis for his new project. He began a series of rebuilds on the car and went to work getting publicity.

In this he was more skillful than P. T. Barnum. Stories popped up almost daily in national magazines. *BUSINESS WEEK* published an article which included a picture of the car with Maria Montez at the wheel. At the time, she was the queen of Universal Pictures "B" adventure movies. The story called the Californian a "tri-wheel, stream-lined, reputedly gas-economical car" which was to be in production by spring of 1946 at the rate of 50 per day. Davis was quoted as saying that the new car would "accept a four-, six-, or eight-cylinder engine." He claimed a top speed of 80 miles an hour with the four-cylinder installed. He also announced a distribution plan, the details of which were not revealed, but which featured a system of drive-in repair shops. A faulty engine would be removed (the change could be done in 14 minutes according to Davis) and a rental power plant installed. The owner could return later to pick up his refurbished engine.

Since the weight of the entire car was given as only 1,000 pounds, Davis' proposed eight-cylinder engine would have had to be super-lightweight. No engine of that size was ever mounted in a Davis by the manufacturer. As far as top speed figures, neither this nor later Davis models ever went faster than 75 miles per hour.

Davis proceeded to gather a crew of young aircraft workers who were eager to be part of this exciting try at breaking into what must be the most competitive of endeavors … automaking. These young men were willing to work on a delayed-wage basis, while holding down regular jobs elsewhere. One source said they were promised double their $6 per hour salaries if the venture was successful, but nothing if it failed.

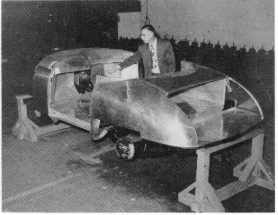

Davis and Davis in hotel parking lot.

Budd Patterson headed the repair department for Seattle dealer Calhoun.

Davis took over an empty plant in Van Nuys and set up a rudimentary assembly line. He began operations. As a promotion he built a racetrack behind the plant where races and gymkhanas could be held.

The crew dismantled the Californian and designer Joe Charipar made detail drawings of it to be used in the production machine. The original car had been a three-seater - the new prototype was widened to take four in the single seat which was 54 inches wide. Wheelbase was lengthened from the Californian's normal 101-1/2 to 108 inches.

Ground clearance was increased an inch-and-a-half from the earlier car's road-hugging six-inches. Overall length was now 15 feet and the car stood only five feet high with its removable top in place. It was extremely low-slung for the time. New features included a 72-inch long wraparound Plexiglas™ windshield and a removable top which was claimed to be strong enough to withstand a rollover. Aluminum took the place of the Californian's steel for the body shell.

The most obvious changes in appearance were elimination of the Californian's separate rear fenders, which had bulged outside the body lines, and disappearance of the chromed front grille. The body was widened to 60 inches at the back to make a smooth curve from nose-to-rear. The headlights were concealed under cable-operated flaps ala the Cord 810.

Davis' first plan for the body was to use aluminum panels bolted to the sub-frame, providing easy and low-cost replacement in case of dents. Advertising drawings showed how the panels could be replaced individually without a costly session at the body shop. The cost factor involved in stamping the flanges for the overlapping body segments made that idea impossible and the cars were all built using panels rivetted to the framework. Use of steel for the bodies would have been cheaper by almost $100 per car, but the weight differential would have hurt performance.

The handsome Davis brochures abounded in novel features. The car's radio was designed to slide into a dash compartment where it mated with power terminals. Out-of the car it could be switched to operate on its own battery as a portable. Seats were covered at the factory with a heavy cotton muslin and the customer could order from a choice of seat covers if he chose. Proposed optional equipment included a built-in jacking system and a tachometer.

Gary Davis had no equal when it came to promotion. He announced a complete line of models including, beside the basic four-passenger coupe, a long-wheelbase sedan seating seven, a panel delivery, a station wagon and a military vehicle. Two of the last model were actually built. They carried a jeep-like body mounted on a beefed-up chassis. Davis also displayed a mock-up of the long wheelbase sedan. It was merely a normal chassis lengthened a foot-and-a-half to allow for a rear seat with a dummy wood-and-plaster body mounted on it. This created great interest, but Davis engineers admitted privately that such a large-size car could not have been built without much redesign work.

A major feature of the car, of course, was the basic three-wheel design. Although the car could be rocked with one hand, it was so stable that Davis delighted in barreling over railroad tracks at top speed, while waving his arms aloft. He also enjoyed cutting figure-eights at speeds which left great streaks of rubber all over the test area without rolling over.

A major advertising point was the fact that use of only three wheels meant a 25 percent reduction in cost for the already low-priced 5:50-15 tires. The Davis had a turning circle of 13 feet, about half that of a Ford or Chevrolet of the period, and parallel parking in a space only inches longer than the Davis itself was a one-pass affair. The lone front wheel was mounted in an aircraft-type yoke suspended by dual coil springs and was canted at a two-degree angle from vertical for better control.

The first prototype used Kinmont disc brakes, an aftermarket accessory designed for Ford cars, but these were replaced on the later units by standard Ford Bendix brakes to cut costs. Coil springing was used all around, the frame was of tubing and the engine was a four-cylinder 133 cubic-inch Hercules rated at 57 horsepower. Later cars used a larger Continental 162 cubic-inch four which gave 63 horsepower.

The tubing frame was dropped in the interest of cost savings and was replaced by a more conventional channel unit. Semi-elliptic rear springs took the place of the coils to cure the extreme mushiness. Davis engineer Harry Morrow urged Davis to use a fiberglass body in place of the aluminum panels, which were formed by Zeke Kin, a metal fabricator.

All of this redesign work took time, and while his crew was busy in the shop, Davis was busy with the promotion. Late in 1947, he surfaced in the news media, this time better financed and with the new car ready for display to prospective investors. Davis claimed to have spent almost $50,000 on performance testing, tooling design, assembly line layouts and so on. He had reverted to an old idea in automaking; he would assemble the car from sub-assemblies which he would contract for. Davis told the press that this plan would take advantage of the hundreds of small shops in Southern California which were already tooled up from war contracts and which were eager to be part of his operation.

That the public was interested was obvious. After the first showing of the prototype, Davis had received over 30,000 inquiries from all over the country. More important, over 200 would-be dealers had bought franchises to sell the car, paying the Davis Motor Car Company a total of something like one million dollars for what in most cases amounted to a contract, a box of beautifully printed brochures and the right to display the Davis crest, a shield whose quarters contained a bear, a stylized front wheel, a flattened letter "D" and what looks at first glance, like four lemons.

This illustration shows the technical features of the three-wheel Davis car.

The 1985 Pulse is a GCRV, which translates as "Ground Cruising Recreational Vehicle." Two passengers sit tandem-style in its fiberglass body. It is 194 inches long and 54 inches high and uses a motorcycle engine. A deluxe interior was optional. The Pulse weighed 1,050 pounds and gave over 70 miles to the gallon.

The Martin Scootmobile was designed by Charles H. Martin and built in Springfield, Massachusetts in 1921 and 1922. It had a two-cylinder engine.

The 1976 Urbasport Tri-Magnum was among several three-wheelers that HOME MECHANIX publications sold plans for. They included 13 drawings in an 80-page booklet, and over 100 how-to photos.

The Trimuter was originally featured on the cover of MECHANIX ILLUSTRATED magazine in February 1980. Quincy-Lynn Enterprises of Phoenix, Arizona marketed this vehicle as a kit for gas or electric power. Over 21,000 sets of plans were sold the first year.

In England, three-wheel cars have long been taxed at the more favorable rate used for motorcycles. This explained the popularity of the famous Morgan Super Sports, a three-wheeler of the 1930s. Several different types of motorcycle engines were used to power these race and fast sports cars.

The Space Shuttle Inn, located near the Kennedy Space Center (Spaceport USA) uses a futuristic-looking three-wheel car as a promotional vehicle. It is featured on the postcard that somebody sent to Wally Wray, a well-known three-wheel car enthusiast from Argyle, Wisconsin.

257

Top: The Ceres was a distinctive three-wheel car design by Creative Cars Corporation of Rockford, Illinois. It had a $13,875 price tag in 1983.

Right: William Schmitt of Xenia, Ohio made his car from salvaged auto parts and an old motorcycle engine. It cost him $400. He claimed speeds up to 65 miles per hour and 45 miles per gallon economy.

Right: Russ Abrams of Cedarhurst, New York called his car the Rockette. It was a war surplus gas tank with a three horsepower Briggs & Stratton engine. It weighed 230 pounds, went 25 miles per hour and got 100 miles per gallon.

Right: V.G. Clements of Elmwood, Nebraska made a tricycle from a washing machine, a wheel barrow, a bicycle and a windmill. It had a 1/2 horsepower engine that gave 60 to 70 miles per gallon and could go 10 miles per hour.

Left: Featured in a 1950 issue of SCIENCE and MECHANICS was a prop-driven three-wheel car built by Willie Menkenns of Hillsboro, Oregon that looks like a prototype for the Flintstone Flyer.

Left: Robert Taylor of Bridgeport, Connecticut made a three-wheel motor scooter with a four horsepower engine. It did 30 miles per gallon and held two persons.

Ultra Streamliners

The nose of the ALFA B.A.T. car shows the effect that ultra streamlining can have on the contours of an automobile. The quest for a functional, aerodynamic shape that can slip more smoothly through the air stream has resulted in many strange-looking automobiles. This section showcases over 60 years of rolling sculpture.

Fred Bergholt created an ultra streamlined car that looked like a weird Pierce Silver Arrow. The Minneapolis, Minnesota cosmetics maker spent five months and $3,000 building it. Big automakers said the car was too far advanced in design, but then infringed Bergholt's patents. He sued them for $1.5 million, but settled for less.

This streamlined bus was used in an old movie.

Hal Holtom, a British-born automotive consultant, created his streamliner in 1934. It had an unusual "optical illusion" grille design some 40 years before the Op-Art artistic movement evolved. Other strange features included the small windows above the windshield and the light down the center of the roof. The car's side trim was also dramatic and bold-looking. This car was envisioned as the perfect New York City taxicab, but only one prototype was constructed.

The Briggs Manufacturing Company of Detroit, Michigan supplied Ford and Chrysler with car bodies. In 1934, the company produced this experimental streamlined car designed by John Tjaarda. A weird thing about this project was that either front or rear engine locations could be used. A mockup of the car created lots of excitement when seen at the 1934 Chicago World's Fair. In 1935, the first operational rear-engined Briggs car was built.

This mystery car was built in Oakland, California in 1935. Actually, there was very little about it that was truly mysterious. Battery-maker Earl Clifford produced the three-wheel electric vehicle to advertise his battery business. It was eight feet long, four and one-half feet high and cost about a penny-per-mile to run.

New C

George L. Coleman of Littleton, Colorado made a streamliner in 1934. It was based on a Ford and designed to sell for under $1,000. Only five cars like this were made.

The 1936 Morrison was wider at the front and tapered toward the rear. It could hold three people up front, but only two at the rear. The car's steering wheel was under the cowl, in front of the windshield. The car had a periscope for rear vision.

The 1936 Bridges had a single, four-passenger seat near its front and a four-cylinder engine in the rear. Calvin B. Bridge, a professor at the California Institute of Technology said it could do 65 miles per hour.

Richard Crossley built his Aerocoupe in East Haven, Connecticut during 1936. It was a three-wheeler constructed of automobile and airplane parts. He claimed it could speed to 75 miles per hour.

The Arrowhead was designed by W. Everett Miller and built in 1936 by Advance Auto Body Company of Los Angeles, California. It cost $8,000 to make and was used as a promotional vehicle for the Arrowhead Spring Water Company. A rear-mounted Ford V-8 drove through the two front wheels.

The 1937 Pribil looked something like Casper-the-Ghost with wheels. It was designed as a streamlined safety vehicle and camper. The rear wheels were just 14 inches apart, so no differential was needed. It included a davenport, a sink, a table and a refrigerator inside.

Ben Harris was a Chicago industrial designer who created this sports car for himself in 1937. It had a 92 cubic-inch V-8 and could hit 110 miles per hour. It had concealed pop-up headlights and a rear dorsal fin.

The 1937 Airmobile wasn't a car for "air heads." It was designed by the owner of Lewis American Airways as a production prototype incorporating the most advanced ideas in auto design and aircraft construction.

Charles D. Thomas built his dream car in 1939 in Batavia, New York. The streamliner had a one-piece unit body, independent front suspension, padded safety interior and a periscope for viewing the road behind it. Thomas attempted to raise financial backing to produce this car, but failed. He did, however, manage to market the Playboy mini-car after World War II. In August 1940, the aerodynamic Thomas was featured in MOTOR magazine and drew lots of national attention.

This streamlined vehicle was photographed by Mel Jamieson when it was being used to promote sales of movie tickets to a film called "The Freak." We're not sure if this was the name of an early postwar space or horror flick, or if it was actually "The Freaks," a 1932 classic about a traveling sideshow and its unusual performers. The car's spaceship appearance would suggest the former.

The NuGrape soda car was an early productmobile that had a touch of streamlining. It was built on a '29 Chevy chassis by Mercury Body Company.

263

The Phantom Corsair is a famous streamliner designed by Rust Heinz, built by Bohman & Schwartz and later owned by Andy Granatelli, Herb Shriner and Bill Harrah.

The "Flying Wombat" Was Weird

By John Gunnell

The Phantom Corsair had a "tasty" design that really "cut the mustard" with fans of automotive streamlining. This may have been due to the fact that it was styled by Rust Heinz, whose family put mustard, ketchup and other types of foods on many American tables.

The heir to the food fortune was a 23 year old college student when he decided to make his Cord 810 look different than anything else on the roads in 1938. He enjoyed sketching customized versions of production cars. After doing the drawing board work for the Phantom Corsair, he took his plans to Bohman & Schwartz, the Pasadena, California coachbuilders.

Actually, the first visit to Pasadena came in 1936. About a dozen scale models were made. The project was more than a quick custom redo. It cost Heinz $24,000 to build the car. However, he hoped to produce the dream car on a limited-ecdition basis, selling copies to those in his circle of wealthy friends for about $15,000 a pop. Sales brochures were actually printed.

Aircraft-type construction was featured with the Cord's front sub-frame attached to a professionally-fabricated chrome-moly steel chassis frame. For body construction, aluminum body panels were attached to a tube frame.

Safety was stressed along with streamlining. The car held six passengers, with four in the front and two facing backwards in the rear. All were protected by cork and rubber padding. Gauges to monitor oil temperature, manifold vacuum and fuel economy were added, along with a battery charge level indicator, an altimeter, a barometer and a compass. Strangely, though, the car had no rearview mirror.

The Lycoming V-8 from the Cord was modified to produce some 190 horsepower. Top speeds of 115 to 130 miles per hour were reported to various sources. Those sources included the automotive trade magazines of the day, which fell in love with the Phantom Corsair and frequently pictured it.

Its interesting appearance also earned the car a role in the 1938 film "The Young in Heart." It was a comedy about a family of wacky con artists trying to walk the straight

"Young in Heart" was the name of a 1938 motion picture that starred Janet Gaynor, Douglas Fairbanks Jr., Paulette Goddard, Roland Young and the Phantom Corsair. In the 90 minute comedy, the car was called the "Flying Wombat."

and narrow. In the movie, the car even had a wacky name. It was called the "Flying Wombat."

The following year, Heinz signed a contract to showcase the Phantom Corsair at the 1939 edition of the New York World's Fair. That June, while returning from a dance in Greensburg, Pennsylvania, Heinz was a passenger in a car involved in a serious accident. He died the next morning.

His dream car was at the World's Fair when the accident took place. After the event closed in 1940, it was put in a warehouse in Queens, New York where it stayed until 1942. Heinz's brother then gave the car to Louis Maxon, who ran the food firm's Detroit, Michigan advertising agency.

A series of owners followed: An industrialist in Michigan, a doctor in Chicago and then a used car dealership in the Windy City. It finally would up in the Chicago repair shop ran by the Granatelli Brothers, Joe, Vince and Andy. Next, it turned up in Washington, D.C., owned by a staffer from the Truman administration. Then E.G. Studebaker of Bedford, Pennsylvania bought it. In 1951, he sold it to entertainer Herb Shriner.

Shriner owned the car for 20 years. He enjoyed the attention it drew and loved exhibiting it in the New York International Motorsports Shows of the early 1950s. Later, in 1954, he had it restyled by industrial designer Albrecht Goertz. Among the changes it received were a two-tone paint job and an open split-front grille for better cooling.

Late in 1954, Shriner put the car in a Florida auto museum. It stayed there until 1967, partly due to legal entanglements related to personal finances. Ultimately, Shriner proved ownership and recovered the car. Three years later, he was killed in an accident while driving his 1963 Studebaker Avanti. Collector car dealer Tom Barrett then obtained the Phantom Corsair. It was then sold to the Harrah's Automobile Collection in Reno, Nevada.

Harrah's took possession in 1972. It was immediately placed in the collection's in-house restoration facility and restored back to the original Rust Heinz configuration. When the job was done, it looked like the Flying Wombat again.

The B.A.T. 5 was constructed by Nuccio Bertone for Alfa Romeo to explore advanced aerodynamics. B.A.T. meant "Berlina Aerodynamica Tecnica," not "Batmobile." It debuted in July 1953. Streamlining gave the 90 horsepower car a 124 miles per hour top speed. Joe Pryzak of South Bend, Indiana saved it.

The second B.A.T. debuted at the 1954 Turin auto show. It had a crisper front and the strangest-looking tail-fins ever seen. The slots in the fins balanced air pressure. Sports car dealer "Wacky" Arnolt imported the cars here. This one was raced and had the fins removed. It is now restored to original shape.

The 9d was the third B.A.T. car introduced at Turin in spring 1955. The tear-drop-shaped streamliner had smaller fins, headlamp covers and an Alfa-like grille. It is owned by Dr. Gary Kaberle who bought the Italian dream car from a used car lot in 1963 when he was just "sweet 16."

Vans

The van is a handy type of truck that dates way back to the early days of automotive history. It's interesting that the early delivery van evolved into the panel truck, which was displaced by the compact, forward-control type van in the early 1960s. In the late 1960s and early 1970s, custom vans and travel vans were hot market segments. The gas crunch cut into van sales in the mid- to late-1970s, but mini-vans came to the rescue. In this section of WEIRD CARS, we'll take a brief look at some of the unusual things that have been done to different types of vans. We start with a Jeep Fleetvan with barred windows that "copped" our attention. What's the story behind its "arresting" decor? Read on to find out. (Don Fest photo)

The Super Van is one of the most recognizable vans ever built. It has made appearances in eight to 10 different Hollywood motion pictures. Its last starring role was in "Back to the Future II," the 1989 hit starring Michael J. Fox, Christopher Lloyd and Lea Thompson which sent the adventurers traveling through different eras of time in their Delorean. The van was painted up as the Hill Valley Transit bus for that role.

Back in the late 1970s, Tee-Bird Products of Exton, Pennsylvania (a first-class supplier of vintage Ford Thunderbird restoration items) built this weird-looking parts hauler. A Ford Econoline van body was mounted backwards on a car-towing trailer. It had the appearance of a van balanced on center-mounted tandem wheels and attracted quite a bit of attention as it rolled down the highway.

Industrial designer Brooks Stevens, of Mequon, Wisconsin, created two of these prototype vans in the late-1950s. They were based on the Willys-Jeep FC-100 forward-control pickup truck. One was used by industrialist Henry J. Kaiser on his island estate on Michigan's Upper Peninsula. These unique vehicles were the predecessors of all the similar vans that followed in the 1960s.

Concours Motors, Inc. of Milwaukee was Wisconsin's largest Volkswagen and Porsche dealer in the 1960s, but the van that the company used was probably the shortest Volkswagen Bus in captivity. The body was shortened approximately four feet near the center, which gave it a comical look. This photo was taken at the famous Road America race course in Elkhart Lake.

Looking somewhat like Casper the Ghost with wheels, this short-wheelbase Fageol Twin Coach moving van was built for inner-city household moves. Nowadays, the truck belongs to Dan W. Golden, a collector of antique telephones from San Marcos, California. He says it has a 1954 International Harvester Company 8-ton chassis.

The Voyager III concept vehicle from Chrysler combined two separate units. Up front was a three-passenger urban transport module that was only 104 inches long with a 1.6-liter propane fuel engine. The rear unit added a 2.2-liter four-cylinder engine for extra power. With both sections connected, the overall length of the seven-passenger unit is only slightly longer than a contemporary Grand Voyager mini-van.

Who are the two fellows "monkeying" around with the "paddy wagon" that we saw earlier in this section? They are members of a civic organization from New York that uses the vintage van to raise money for charities. The FJ-3A Fleetvan used a Jeep CJ-5 81-inch wheelbase chassis and went into production in 1961. (Don Fest photo)

Going "Ape" for a Good Cause

By "Wild Bill" Bitterman

Look out! It's a raid! The "Keystone '90s Cops" are here to serve up their own unique form of justice on all wrong-doers in the Western New York area.

Since 1969, this zany bunch of police officers and gorillas have been delighting both young and old with their unique showing of madness and mayhem. They were originally banded together by a former cancer patient, Wally Albarella of Depew, New York.

Their means of transportation is a 1961 Willys Fleetvan, which was purchased by Mr. Albarella in 1969. Originally a postal van, this one-of-a-kind vehicle has been completely overhauled by removing the original 134.2 cubic-inch, 75 horsepower, F-head engine and replacing it with a 327 cubic-inch Chevrolet engine with a Turbo-hydramatic 400 transmission and 12-bolt rear end.

The Keystone '90s Cops are a totally non-profit organization, donating all funds to charity. They pull off fake raids and "busts" at weddings, parades, picnics and lawn fetes. All money raised is donated to the American Cancer Society's Roswell Park Clinic.

The organization consists of 14 members, including four gorillas, nine cops and a chicken. Wally's gang is available for all birthday parties and social events. For information write: Wally Albarella, 5836 Transit Road, DePew, N.Y. 14043 or call (715) 681-4137.

Weird Working

Vehicles

A vintage White streamliner truck once used to deliver Labatt's beer in Canada has been restored for promotional purposes. Several photos of this weird, but wonderful tractor-trailer appear here and with a related story that opens the "Working Vehicles" section of WEIRD CARS. The rear of the truck has a hinged door. Display equipment is carried in the trailer. The sleek, curvy lines of the beautiful truck were designed by Count Alexis deSakhnoffsky.

273

The cab of the Labatt's streamliner is strange-looking, although very stylish with its radical curves. The rear wheels of the tractor unit are skirted.

How Do You Spell Relief?
They Spelled It "Labatt's"

By Bruce Tait

For many people in Ontario, Canada during the 1930s, 1940s and 1950s, the sight of a Labatt's streamliner truck rolling down the road in summer meant that relief from the heat was close at hand.

The Labatt's Brewing Company, one of the largest in Canada, used the streamlined trucks to deliver their product to the brewer's retail outlets. Their fleet was in use on the Ontario highways from 1932 to 1955. It provided an image and made Labatt's corporate symbol instantly recognizable.

The tractor chassis used for these streamliners was produced by the White Motor Company. The trailer chassis were manufactured by Fruehauf. Count Alexis deSakhnoffsky designed the bodies, which were built by Smith Brothers Bodyworks of Toronto.

It was 1955 when the last of these transports was phased out of operation. They were replaced with conventional tractor and trailer combinations. However, one of the old trucks has been rescued and restored.

Joe and Bob Scott, of London, Ontario, handled the difficult restoration for Labatt's Brewing Company. It took seven years to complete the job, but the Scott brothers' attention to detail resulted in an excellent restoration.

The streamliner tractor chassis is a 1948 White model WA122 of cab-over-engine design. The engine is a White "Mustang" model 150A. It is a six-cylinder type displacing 386 cubic inches and developing 135 horsepower. Bore and stroke are 4 x 5-1/8 inches.

Power is transmitted through a White model 501-B five-speed manual transmission linked to a model 33C single-reduction, single-speed rear axle with a 6.67:1 gear ratio. Steering is handled by a White Wide Track model 30-D I-beam reverse Elliott front axle. Size 9.00 x 20 tires are mounted all around.

The trailer is a Fruehauf single-axle type of low bed configuration. A wood lining is used. It once served to keep the product cool during transit to cities throughout the province.

This streamliner is now officially back in service. It is used as a promotional vehicle for Labatt's Brewing Company at fairs and exhibitions in Ontario. Display equipment is carried inside the trailer.

As a show vehicle the swoopy looking truck doesn't deliver any beer, but it's still a welcome sight to the people of Ontario. It provides them with an opportunity to view the fine truck-building craftsmanship of years gone by.

This 1960 Mercury Comet looks neat as a custom pickup truck. It has all the "trick" custom accessories of that period, such as dummy spot lamps, moon wheel discs, Lakes pipes and cruiser skirts.

An unusual home-made pickup truck is Jim Bryan's 1964 Pontiac GTO. After the car was damaged, the New York State body man added the cargo box. It is made of wood, steel and aluminum with diamond-plate running boards.

American Motors never mass-produced an El Camino-type pickup truck, so this one was built by an AMC enthusiast who did what the factory didn't. It even has an attractive patterned vinyl top.

Proving again that pickup conversions are popular with old car fans, this "Rambler Ranchero" is another example of "American" (American Motors) ingenuity.

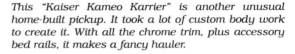

One of the most unusual pickup conversions we've seen is this one built from a Mustang. The full four-passenger Mustang body has been kept intact, with a Ranchero-type cargo box added to the rear.

This "Kaiser Kameo Karrier" is another unusual home-built pickup. It took a lot of custom body work to create it. With all the chrome trim, plus accessory bed rails, it makes a fancy hauler.

"1-Hot-IH" reads the license plate on this ground-hugging, customized International-Harvester Scout pickup from Virginia. The chopped top is designed to keep anyone with a "swelled head" from riding in the cab

A real "home"made slide-in camper takes up the back of this Custom Deluxe 20 Chevrolet pickup. When the owner's wife puts him "out in the dog house" he has room to stretch out. You should see the size of his dog!

Joe C. Pickett is the owner and sponsor of John Wayne's "War Wagon." This truck was custom-built for the actor in 1966. He used it on his Arizona ranch. The four-wheel-drive International Carry All is equipped with a 10,000-pound winch, a roll bar, air-conditioning, an electric rear window and a special five-speed transmission. The roof had to be raised six inches so Wayne could wear his Stetson while riding inside the truck. The name War Wagon comes from the hatch installed in the top, so Wayne could pop through it to shoot his hunting rifle.

You've seen cow lawn ornaments and kitchen gadgets. Here's a cow truck, complete with horns, udders, a tail, a cow bell, cow seat covers and a cow horn to call her husband "Bull." Although this mini-pickup looks like something that should have been custom-made for actor John Wayne, it actually belongs to Richard Pollard, of Salem, Illinois, who built it for reasons "udderwise" left unsaid.

This piggyback transporter was seen at work hauling a race car at Domora, California in 1960. The truck also appeared at other West Coast racing events in 1961. It was dubbed the "Cheetah." Combining the chassis and the cab from an El Camino pickup (bobbed at the cowl line) it was featured in several car magazines such as MOTOR LIFE, CAR and DRIVER and MECHANIX ILLUSTRATED. Side air scoops ducted cool air to the power plant behind the front wheels. A Corvette V-8 bored to 300 cubic inches gave a top speed of 100 miles per hour.

The Cheetah high-speed transporter was built by Norm Holikamp and Don Allen. In 1961, they estimated the truck's value to be $16,000. It was patterned after Mercedes' factory transporter (inset photo) for their SLR race cars and limited-production was envisioned. Dean Moon, the inventor of Moon discs, later had a Cheetah. Vintage racing buff James M. Degnan obtained this vehicle from Moon's widow. It is now mostly restored and will soon be used to carry his Lotus 51 and Allard K-2 to vintage races.

This looks like a motor home built for the "Little King" of comic strip notoriety. It is short, but has luxury fitting a king with its 1960 Cadillac front end. If the mini-monarch brings along some of his taller friends, the roof on the rear body unit has been constructed to raise like a pop-up camper top. It is seen here at an auction in Rockford, Illinois.

How's this for a strange and unusual working vehicle. It's a 1941 Cadillac Carved Cathedral hearse. Meteor of Piqua, Ohio was the coach builder. It weighs 6,000 pounds and stretches 22 feet long. The hearse was in service from April 1941 to sometime in 1965. It changed hands several times before Bernie Brown found it sitting in 1978. It was sitting in a field in Round Lake, Illinois. The Hickory Hills collector replaced the engine in 1979.

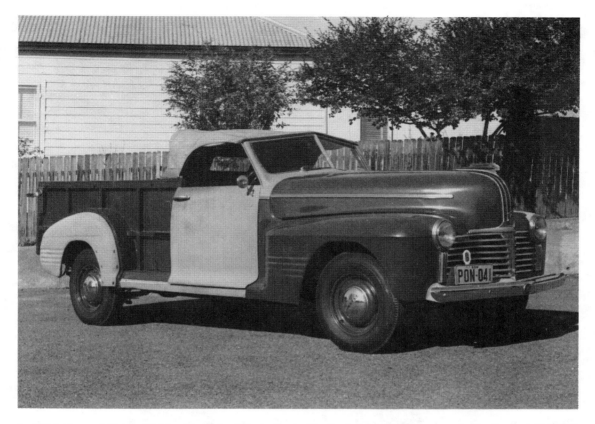

In 1941, General Motors-Holden Limited, of Australia, built a limited number of open-cab, Pontiac based "Utes" for use by the Australian Royal Air Force in World War II. They were constructed from closed-bodied passenger car dies and featured steel pickup beds with wood framing and particle sideboards.

At least three 1941 Pontiac Australian Utes still exist. This example of the special military vehicle was owned by Allen Seymour of Australia. All 1941 Australian Pontiacs had plain hood-side trim moldings with no wording on them, which was another departure from standard American models.

Ron Paetz of Blue River, Wisconsin owns this unusual working vehicle. It is a 1920 Model T Ford "Depression Tractor." Vehicles such as this one could be built from old Fords, using a kit of special parts, during the Great Depression. They are rare to see today. This one appeared at the Wisconsin Capitol Model T Ford Club's annual "Hill & Valley Rally" in Cross Plains, Wisconsin during September 1990.

"Old Tom" is a vintage truck that is used to pull an antique "Gypsy wagon" in Cornwall, England. Tom and Nancy Hoefert, of Chula Vista, California, snapped this photo while on vacation.

X-Peri men tal Cars

Many automotive inventors have used the letter "X" to code their experimental cars and prototype vehicles. The automotive "X-periments" depicted in these photos revolve around tests of different lighting systems. In the smaller photo, the Chrysler in the foreground and the Plymouth behind it have three headlamps on each side. The Buick behind the Plymouth and the Pontiac at the rear have dual headlamps.

In the larger photo, we see a variety of cars (a Pontiac and a Lincoln) and test units wearing various combinations of multiple headlamps. The Pontiac has 1954 Ohio license plates, though this Chieftain Deluxe station wagon is of earlier 1950s vintage. The Lincoln has a special front plate commemorating the 75th anniversary of General Electric Company.

This section of WEIRD CARS covers non-factory prototype vehicles that experimented with a variety of "far out" ideas.

The Tri-Phibian of 1935 was weird in many ways. It had three wheels and was designed to operate on land, or water, or in the air. Inventor Constantios H. Vlachos was seriously injured when the car blew up during a demonstration in front of the Library of Congress.

Driven by a mechanism placed between the large, but close-together front wheels, the electric-powered 1897 Barrows was steered by bicycle handlebars. Sleigh runners, for winter, were $10 extra.

Constructed in the early 1980s, the Briggs & Stratton car had a hybrid engine that ran on both gasoline and electricity. The gas engine was for long trips, while the electric motors could be used for quiet, economical shopping excursions.

Brooks Stevens Design Associates, of Mequon, Wisconsin, designed the Briggs & Stratton hybrid electric car. The four rear wheels helped support the extra weight of the heavy batteries used to supply power to the electric motors. The car is still in existence at the Brooks Stevens Automotive Museum in Mequon.

Like Briggs & Stratton's hybrid, the 1907 Pratt had six wheels. They were needed for a different reason. They supported the long frame of the 168-inch wheelbase car. At the extreme rear were the two drive wheels. Both the front and center wheels could be steered. Only one of these cars was built.

Before four-wheeled cars became "conventional," auto inventors experimented with different numbers of wheels in various formats. The 1907 Autocycle looked somewhat like a motorcycle with "training wheels." The balance wheels on either side were not needed, except when it was traveling very slow.

Perhaps the strangest thing about the $5,000 Reeves Sexto auto was that it cost $1,800 more than the Octoauto. Two of these cars were built in 1912. Both were different. One was an Octoauto with one axle removed. The second was a Stutz with an axle added. Reeves gave up his auto experiments after 1912.

The Octoauto

An Appreciation By Elbert Hubbard

Milton O. Reeves was a born experimenter who tried out various different automobile ideas. One of his beliefs was that the comfort level in a car was directly related to the number of wheels it had. On that basis, his 1911 Octoauto should have been twice as comfortable as most competitor's products.

In the good old days when I used to take the cattle to the Chicago Stock Yards, I carried a long hickory pole, a basket of grub, and much enthusiasm.

On long runs, my home was in the caboose for perhaps three days and three nights. It was a sad day, however, when, instead of a regular, genuine caboose, they bundled the merry stockmen into a dinkey.

The difference between a dinkey and a caboose is that a caboose has four wheels on each side, and a dinkey has only four wheels altogether, one on each corner. The dinkey's business is to bounce, jounce, jolt, jar and jerk, and make a puncture in your vocabulary.

A wheel is a plan of continually hitting the rail. The Pullmans, it was, who discovered that when you hit the rail in twelve places in running a car, you greatly reduce the amount of jar and the wear and tear both on the rails and the rolling-stock.

A car having twelve wheels is considered doubly safe as one having eight.

A wheel lives its life exactly as a man does his. A man will stand a great number of raps and kicks supplied by Fate, provided they are distributed over a long period of time, but if you come to concentrate them in a few years, or a few months, or a few days, you destroy the man by destroying his nerve fabric.

In the Reeves Octoauto, the load is distributed over eight wheels, instead of being concentrated on four. In a four-wheeled automobile, a wheel at each corner carries one-fourth of the load. In case of an imperfection in the road, the sudden dropping down into a rut, one wheel may for an instant carry half of the load, and it is this sudden jolt and burden that causes tire trouble. You get enough of these tremendous pressures in a day, and your tire reaches its limit and explodes with a loud R.G. Dun and Company report. If you are running fast, you may lose control and the ditch, always waiting, gets you. So the proposition is, if you can save your wheels from these severe jolts which will occasionally come through dropping into a rut, you are going to prolong the life of the tire, the life of the car and the life of its occupants.

When you break your leg or sprain your ankle, it is not on account of long, slow service. It is because you get a sudden twist or smash. Just so with tires — it is a jam and jar that does the business.

It is figured out on a reasonable basis that by the use of eight wheels, eight times the ordinary service is obtainable. If the car were always evenly balanced on four wheels, your tires would live probably ten times as long as they do now; but in turning corners and dropping into ruts, and hitting high places, a severe shock has to be met by your wheels. It is the accumulated results of these shocks that lays you up at the inopportune time.

I had the pleasure of taking a ride in an Octoauto in Chicago. The driver was a reckless fellow, and the wonder is that we were not pinched and given the limit by the judge; but fortunately our driver picked streets that no other auto with a sane chauffeur would attempt to navigate.

Chicago not only has some of the best pavement in the world, but I believe it can safely claim the booby-prize for the worst.

The worst pavement possible is in the Nicholson Blocks, where time gets the better of their ego. A busted-up Nicholson pavement is absolutely the end of the limit. We took Nicholson pavement, which was laid in Eighteen Hundred Eighty-five, at the rate of twenty-five miles an hour, absolutely oblivious of the ruts. Very few of these ruts were over three feet, but so evenly was the weight divided that we were on terra cotta most of the time, and the wear and tear and jar were distributed, for before one wheel could really go down and hit the bottom of a rut, the wheel behind it was to the rescue on firm footing and relieved the strain. This taking ruts and bumps without jar is something that no man can possibly appreciate who has not experienced a ride in an Octoauto.

In this thing of running over a surface filled with ruts that are from three to six inches deep, and yet experiencing scarcely any bounce, jounce, jar, or jolt, two big items are obtainable. One is ease to the passenger, and the next is, length of life to the auto.

The whole arrangement is very simple and is a shock-absorber beyond the dreams of the neurotic.

THE REEVES "OCTOAUTO" Car is conventional throughout, except the four additional carrying wheels. Steers and controls exactly the same as a four-wheeled car.

The only car in the world built on the principle of a Pullman Palace-Car.

The Easiest Car in the World on Tires.

Tire authorities say that tires on an Octoauto should give eight times the ordinary service.

This truly wonderful car is manufactured and sold by M.O. REEVES, COLUMBUS, INDIANA. President Peoples Savings and Trust Company, Vice-President Reeves Pulley Company who will be glad to send full descriptive pamphlet containing prices to those interested. Agents wanted.

Funny Car Facts

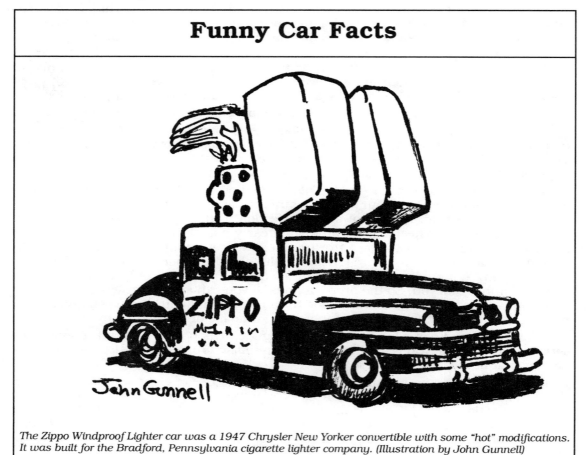

The Zippo Windproof Lighter car was a 1947 Chrysler New Yorker convertible with some "hot" modifications. It was built for the Bradford, Pennsylvania cigarette lighter company. (Illustration by John Gunnell)

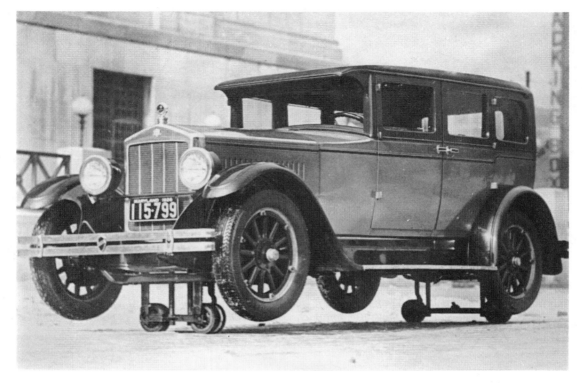

If you think the Octoauto had lots of wheels, the Parkmobile-equipped New York Six would really amaze you. It had 12 wheels, but eight were small dolly wheels that lowered hydraulically. The raised car could then be moved, sideways, into tight parking spaces. This gimmick never sold very well.

Another automotive experimenter was J.B. MacDuff of Brooklyn, New York. His "pneumoslito" (German for "air sled") had a large propeller at the rear. It was driven by a four-horsepower engine and could do 25 miles per hour. He talked of building a larger version that would run on land or sea.

The Tasco Special was built in 1948 by Derham Body Company, which built many prewar classic cars. It was designed by the great classic car stylist Gordon Buehrig. The airplane-like Plexiglas roof had removeable panels like a modern T-top.

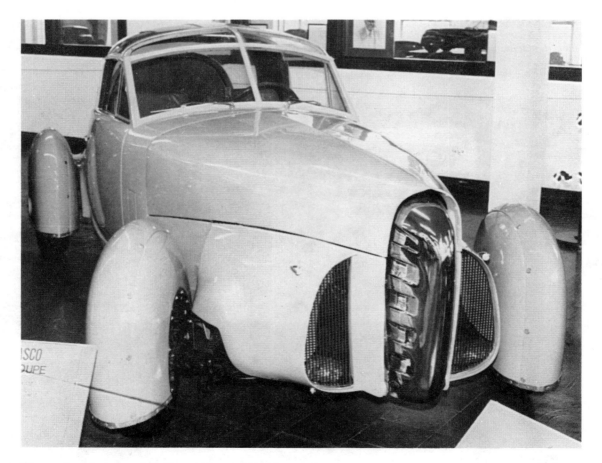

Other unique features of the Tasco Special included its aircraft-inspired cigar-shaped body and front fenders that turned with the front wheels. It had a Mercury V-8 and was designed to sell for $7,500. Tasco stood for The American Sports Car Company.

In 1908, a Waterloo, Iowa company invented the Caldwell "Iron Horse." It was a power plant that attached to the front of a horse drawn buggy to make it a horseless carriage. It had a hollow, moving piston sliding back and forth in a stationary cylinder head.

Joe Kulage, of St. Louis, Missouri, invented a weird-looking conveyance in 1896 or 1897. It carried four passengers between two large wagon wheels, with the riders facing in opposite directions. The driver did not have to worry about tipping over, but making turn signals was a "bear."

This weird-looking car was photographed by Mel Jameson in Michigan. Judging from the background, the time was in the early postwar years. The vehicle was made of wood and aluminum. It looked like an oversized dodge-'em car.

Rear view of this wood-and-aluminum car looks something like a "shoe box Ford" with its front clip removed. Both the front and rear tires on the vehicle were fully enclosed.

The Luxor looks as if it was inspired by a Charlton Heston movie featuring gladiators and Roman chariots. C.R. Harris designed the odd-looking buggy around 1900. It had a four-horsepower engine, bicycle tires and tiller steering. This car was never produced.

Looking like a prop from a Jules Verne science fiction tale, the Tiffany was a $750 electric car offered in 1913 to 1914. Few were ever made from the start of the company in October 1913 and its end in March 1914.

With a name like Dollwet, you have to wonder about this little contraption built in 1903. The seat was made from a soap box and was so tall that 16-year-old John Dollwet had to use his feet to steer his car.

Here's a great vehicle for folks who are into basket weaving. The Electriquette was made in Los Angeles, California from 1914 to 1915. These electric-powered vehicles were rented to San Diego Exhibition visitors for $1 per hour. Around 200 were built.

Harry S. Parker's car used parts from 17 different vehicles. The Ellsworth, Maine resident worked eight hours per day for 17 months to build it. (Maybe 17 was his favorite number). The body framing was of steel, sheathed with oak, with 24-gauge black iron outer panels attached. The rear-mounted engine could speed it up to 85 miles per hour.

Yank Tank

The term "Yank Tank" is commonly used to describe a fast, flashy, finny American car of the 1950s. However, this description also applies to the huge and unusual vehicle that you'll find in this section of WEIRD CARS ... the 1940 Snow Cruiser, seen here on the main street of a small Ohio city during a cross country delivery trip.

The Snow Cruiser caused quite a stir as it crossed the country from Illinois to Massachusetts by land. Crowds turned out along the route to see the weird vehicle, which was designed to serve as a mobile station for explorers.

Snow Cruiser: It's All Yours ... Go Get It

By Bob Lichty

Much information about Antarctica was generated from Admiral Richard E. Byrd's expeditions. The trips were carefully organized, lavishly financed and well-equipped to permit the explorer to make many scientific discoveries.

On November 15, 1939 Byrd led his third expedition on a visit to the polar regions. Sponsored by the United States government, his group was known as the United States Antarctic Service. Its mission was to renew the attack upon the unknown regions of the 4,000,000 square miles of Antarctica.

The project was largely financed by a $350,000 congressional appropriation and was outfitted by various governmental departments. The expedition sailed from Boston Harbor with a party of 55 men, plus 140 dogs and 20 puppies for sled dog service. It moved through the Panama Canal to New Zealand for refueling and then went on to the Ross Sea barrier in the early part of January, 1940.

In addition to two land camps, the expedition was able to make use of a mobile base specifically known as "The Snow Cruiser." This huge vehicle was designed to roll across uncharted ice fields on 10-foot tires. It could climb polar mountains and slide down the other side on its smooth ribbed steel belly. More than 55 feet long, 20 feet wide and 15 feet high and weighing 75,000 pounds when completely equipped, the giant vehicle could traverse 15-foot crevasses in the ice. It accommodated a crew of four to five men with a modern laboratory. It had living facilities similar to a modern motorhome. The Snow Cruiser was also designed to carry a five-passenger Beachcraft stagger-wing airplane on its back.

The vehicle was conceived by Dr. Thomas C. Poulter, scientific director of the Armour Institute of Technology in Chicago, Illinois who was second in command during Byrd's second expedition. He had participated in an exhausting rescue of Byrd.

This vividly illustrated the need for a specialized vehicle for Antarctic transportation and survival. Upon returning to the United States, Dr. Poulter began work on the idea of a Snow Cruiser.

Requiring two years from drafting board to final assembly by the Pullman Company of Chicago, the Snow Cruiser was built with relatively few problems. Construction of the all-steel framework began in the Pullman shops on August 8, 1940. It was then sheathed in a steel skin on all surfaces. The bottom was made of 16-gauge sheet steel welded directly to I-beam frame members which protruded sufficiently to act as runners for the vehicle. 14-gauge sheet was used on each of the curved ends, while 28-gauge metal was used on the sides. Since the Snow Cruiser had to have steel that would give maximum strength, minimum weight and high resistance to impact and low temperatures, its designers selected Inland Hi-Steel. This was a high-strength, low-alloy steel that saved thousands of pounds of dead weight.

The vehicle was powered by two diesel-electric generators. This type of drive was selected because of its flexibility and history of performance in buses and locomotives. Each General Electric generator was directly connected to a Cummins Diesel engine. A General Electric series-type traction motor of 75 horsepower was mounted in the hub of each wheel through flexible couplings with 50:1 gear reductions. Control of the four motors gave the operator up to 30 drive combinations with the two generators. Power could be transmitted directly to any of the four wheels or via any combination of them. The Snow Cruiser could attain 30 miles per hour and had sufficient power to traverse 35-percent grades.

The four three-ton wheels and two spare rims were manufactured by the Whiting Corporation of Harvey, Illinois. They were made entirely of welded Inland Hi-Steel. Each wheel was then machined to a close tolerance to receive anti-friction bearings. The wheels measured 66-inches inside tire diameter. The Timken tapered roller bearings were the largest wheel bearings ever made with a 24-inch inside diameter and 32-inch outside diameter. Each carried a 19,000-pound load.

Goodyear Tire and Rubber Company of Akron, Ohio got the task of coming up with tires for the 37-ton giant. Goodyear had already built a number of 10-foot tires for Gulf Refining Company to use on a large amphibious car for marshland exploration in Louisiana. By adding eight more plies for strength, Goodyear came up with a tire strong enough for the 37-ton vehicle without retooling. The surface of Antarctica was very granular, so no special tread was required.

With a 34.5 inch cross section, the tires weighed 750 pounds each. They had 250-pound inner tubes carrying 15-20 pounds of air. Each tire's pressure was shown on the instrument panel of the Snow Crusier and could be adjusted from the cockpit as well. Since rubber freezes at about 75 degrees below zero, exhaust heat was used to warm the tires when the vehicle was not moving. When mobile, the tires themselves generated enough heat to keep from freezing.

One of the Snow Cruiser's most unique features was the manner in which it could traverse crevasses in the ice. Maneuverability, in general, was good. An elaborate system of hydraulics from Hydraulic Controls, Incorporated took care of steering. With use of these controls, the 55-foot vehicle had a turning radius of only 30 feet with all wheels steering. Operating at 15,000-pounds of pressure, the hydraulic rams eliminated all chance of mechanical linkage type failure.

Hydraulic tie bars and check valves maintained alignment and steering control. Hycon Power Hydraulic Brakes were used on the vehicle because of the advantages of a closed system. It prevented the condensation that might be found in an air brake system. Each wheel was equipped with its own hydraulic jack exerting a force of 40,000 pounds. Hycon Power Hydraulic Storage Batteries held reserve hydraulic power in case of emergency. Acco chain and TruLay pre-formed rope were used for additional emergency braking and for winching the giant vehicle out of tight situations. The unusual rope was also used to winch the piggy-back airplane up a 30-foot ramp to the roof of the Snow Cruiser.

Standard Oil Company of Indiana developed a light diesel fuel and special oils and lubricants for the severe weather conditions. The Snow Cruiser carried 2,500-gallons of diesel fuel, enough for a 5,000-mile journey. Another 1,000-gallons of gasoline were available for the airplane.

The finish on the Snow Crusier had to be as tough as the vehicle itself and Armstrong Paint and Varnish Company was selected to come up with a bright red paint. The color scheme was chosen so the vehicle could be easily spotted from the air. Silver, orange and black stripes were Armour Institute colors.

On October 24, 1940 the Snow Cruiser was finished. It faced a 1,021-mile land trip to Boston, Massachusetts, where it would begin its ocean voyage. Even Dr. Poulter was not familiar with the feel or controls of the vehicle. Chicago traffic, narrow city streets, and the strange nature of the vehicle made the first few miles of driving difficult. Bugs began to show up during the trip. However, after fixing faulty hydraulic lines and loose connections, the crew made it to Gary, Indiana by October 26.

Testing was done on the sand dunes near Gary and the vehicle performed flawlessly. On October 28, a high-pressure line blew. This sent the Snow Cruiser through a bridge rail and into a creek bed, damaging two wheel motors. It continued on to Akron, Ohio for spare tires. It then went to Erie, Pennsylvania for repairs on the motors. By time the machine went across the New York state border, most of the bugs had been worked out of it.

The Snow Cruiser created a stir wherever it went. Crippled children were ushered through it. Church services were interrupted. In Farmington, Massachusetts, 20 miles from Boston, a 7,500 car traffic jam developed. The Snow Cruiser was particularly tricky to drive through many of Boston's narrow old roads and bridges.

On October 12, the Snow Crusier pulled up on Boston's Army Wharf, beside the the vessel North Star which was to haul it to Antarctica. To make it fit aboard the boat, the tail section of the crusier had to be removed with cutting torches. It was loaded and set to sea on November 15, 1940.

Byrd's three-year expedition was terminated after the first 12 months due to war conditions around the world. The Snow Cruiser was left behind under the assumption the explorers would soon be back. It was not seen again for nearly 30 years.

In 1969, Dr. Poulter announced that the vehicle had been found at the Little America base camp in Antarctica. It was under 12 feet of ice. Poulter noted that the Snow Cruiser was still operable and ready for use. So, if you are looking for the ultimate collector vehicle to wow the folks at Hershey or Iola next year, why not just run down to Antarctica with an ice pick? You can bring the Snow Cruiser back and do a little restoration on it. Who knows, maybe the folks at Goodyear could make you up a set of new tires; maybe even wide whitewalls.

(Research Material and Photos Courtesy Dave Harrison and Dave Russ, Goodyear Tire & Rubber Company, Akron, Ohio).

High-visibility "American Beauty" red enamel was used to protect the Snow Cruiser's body. It had silver and black "racing" stripes. Cruising speeds of 30 miles per hour were achievable.

Zany Cars
Zany Cars
Zany Cars

During the 1970s, a series of three zany automobiles were created for Manufacturers Hanover Trust of New York City. These "Anycars" were built from the parts of various makes and models of automobiles. They were designed to drive home the fact that MHT's banks would make auto loans for practically any type of car.

A weird thing to note is that Manufacturer's Hanover Trust spelled the name of the cars three different ways. The first was the Any Car I, the second was the AnyCar II and the last was the ANYCAR III.

Seen above (and later inside this chapter) is the ANYCAR III. It was designed by customizer George Barris and featured an amalgamation of parts from some 40 different auto makes and models mated to the body of a 1974 Volkswagen station wagon.

It's certainly the perfect vehicle to open up this "Zany Cars" section.

The Any Car I was built in 1970. It was originally called the "ForChevAmChrysVagen," but the name Any Car was easier for people to remember it by. The main body was that of a Volkswagen Beetle, but the tailfins were from a Chrysler 300 letter car. Parts from over 22 cars were used in its construction.

AnyCar II was as daringly distinctive as its predecessor. Again featuring "something for everyone" styling, it incorporated parts from 50 automobiles dating from prewar to modern. The dominant component was a 1929 Hudson body. Other pieces came from a Cadillac Eldorado and a Plymouth Valiant.

ANYCAR III was as visually dynamic as its two predecessors. It was an amalgamation of parts from some 40 different makes and models of automobiles mated to the body of a 1974 Volkswagen station wagon. Noted customizer George Barris designed the car. Before you flip to the next page in this book, write a list of the cars you think donated parts to ANYCAR III.

Leaving the ANYCAR III for a moment, here's another Volkswagen-inspired zany-mobile. The famous Wrought Iron VW was created by artist Joe Gomez. This photo of the unusual example of automotive art dates back to 1971, although mini-skirts are said to be coming back into fashion today.

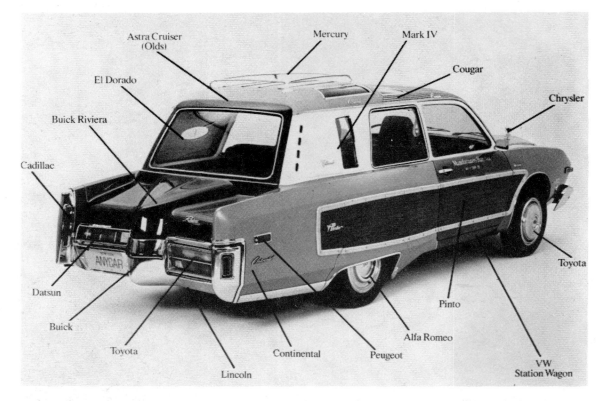

Astra Cruiser (Olds) · Mercury · Mark IV · Cougar · Chrysler · El Dorado · Buick Riviera · Cadillac · Toyota · Datsun · Buick · Toyota · Lincoln · Continental · Peugeot · Alfa Romeo · Pinto · VW Station Wagon · ANYCAR

Here is a photo of the ANYCAR III that answers our challenge on the previous page. It shows which makes and models some of the components used on the promotional car came from. A brand new feature of Manufacturer Hanover Trust's third zany-mobile was a four-speed, battery-powered 27-inch-wide "Mini-Anycar" below the hood. This small vehicle was designed for short-range travel.

This 1966 Corvair convertible may be the highest-flying motor vehicle ever seen. The photograph was acquired from a Corvair enthusiast in Texas who obtained it from a United States Astronaut. Apparently, the Corvair was one of his favorite vehicles. He felt that, because of its prominence in styling and engineering, it should be placed in a favorable perspective within the Space Shuttle Program.

Extravaganza Limousines, Incorporated of Brooklyn, New York has embarked on the development of a series of unusual limousines that embody the ultimate in design, technology and luxury. This is their 1992 Chevrolet Corvette ZR-1 stretch model.

1993 500 SEL MERCEDES BENZ SUPER STRETCH

1993 LS400 LEXUS SUPER STRETCH

1957 CHEVY SUPER STRETCH

Four additional models are offered by Extravaganza Limousines to permit their customers to enjoy their "ultimate fantasy on wheels." The six-window model is the 1993 "747 Jumbo Stretch." As you can see, it's so big it needs a telephone pole, rather than an antenna, for cellular phone reception (only kidding). Below it, left to right, are the 1993 Mercedes 500 SEL Super Stretch; the 1993 Lexus LS400 Super Stretch and the 1957 Chevy Super Stretch.

Look at this vehicle closely and you'll see that something's "a foot" on its roof. Created by the Lincoln Towing Service of Seattle, Washington, it is a genuine "Toe Truck."

"This is what happens when you mess with a laser," says historian Don Wood, who sent this photo to us. The car is owned by the William F. Harrah Automobile Foundation, of Reno, Nevada. Apparently, it was designed for exhibitions at new-car shows to demonstrate the inner workings of a Chevrolet. Similar cars have also been built for "trick" scenes in movies, where cars split apart to squeeze through narrow tunnels or around objects in their path.